T0316509

Cambridge Elements ≡

Elements in Twenty-First Century Music Practice
edited by
Simon Zagorski-Thomas
London College of Music, University of West London

CHINESE STREET MUSIC

Complicating Musical Community

Samuel Horlor
Yunnan University

CAMBRIDGE
UNIVERSITY PRESS

CAMBRIDGE
UNIVERSITY PRESS

University Printing House, Cambridge CB2 8BS, United Kingdom

One Liberty Plaza, 20th Floor, New York, NY 10006, USA

477 Williamstown Road, Port Melbourne, VIC 3207, Australia

314–321, 3rd Floor, Plot 3, Splendor Forum, Jasola District Centre,
New Delhi – 110025, India

79 Anson Road, #06–04/06, Singapore 079906

Cambridge University Press is part of the University of Cambridge.

It furthers the University's mission by disseminating knowledge in the pursuit of
education, learning, and research at the highest international levels of excellence.

www.cambridge.org
Information on this title: www.cambridge.org/9781108822930
DOI: 10.1017/9781108913232

© Samuel Horlor 2021

First published 2021

A catalogue record for this publication is available from the British Library.

ISBN 978-1-108-82293-0 Paperback
ISSN 2633-4585 (online)
ISSN 2633-4577 (print)

Chinese Street Music

Complicating Musical Community

Elements in Twenty-First Century Music Practice

DOI: 10.1017/9781108913232
First published online: April 2021

Samuel Horlor
Yunnan University
Author for correspondence: Samuel Horlor, samhorlor@protonmail.com

Abstract: Musical community is a notion commonly evoked in situations of intensive collective activity and fervent negotiation of identities. Passion Square shows, the daily singing of Chinese pop classics in parks and on street corners in the city of Wuhan have an ambivalent relationship with these ideas. They inspire modest outward signs of engagement and are guided by apparently individualistic concerns; singers are primarily motivated by making a living through the relationships they build with patrons and reflection on group belonging is of lesser concern. How do these orientations help complicate the foundations of typical musical community discourses? This Element addresses community as a quality rather than as an entity to which people belong, exploring its ebbs and flows as associations between people, other bodies and the wider street music environment intersect with its various theoretical implications. A de-idealised picture of musical community better acknowledges the complexities of everyday musical experiences.

Keywords: musical community, street music, Chinese pop, Wuhan, space

ISBNs: 9781108822930 (PB), 9781108913232 (OC)
ISSNs: 2633-4585 (online), 2633-4577 (print)

Contents

1 Introduction

In early 2020, the Chinese city of Wuhan was the first place to live through unprecedented developments soon to become common across the globe, as tight restrictions were placed on many aspects of life – particularly public-space life – in response to the spread of coronavirus disease 2019 (COVID-19). It also became the first centre of another impending worldwide phenomenon, the flurry of expressions of togetherness and solidarity that circulated through traditional media and online in the face of the virus. Musical encouragements for an embattled Wuhan to muster its resilience and 'hang on in there' (*Wuhan jiayou*) were joined by a new impetus for affirmation of local identities. Nostalgic Wuhan-dialect evocations of ordinary city experiences were at the heart of songs such as 'Hanyangmen huayuan' (Hanyang Gate Garden) by local singer-songwriter Feng Xiang (Zhang 2020: 14–15). This folk-idiom composition (*minyao*) for guitar and voice, written a few years earlier but fully taking off during the crisis, holds up the small patch of green space at Hanyang Gate as symbolic of an old Wuhan encroached on by wider modernity; it also makes reference to other places of local significance, especially Minzhu Lu, the road that links the garden with Hubu Xiang, now a partly tourist-orientated street food lane a few minutes' walk away. The evocation of an exclusive local belonging could hardly be more direct:

现在的民主路每天都人挨人
These days, there are always people everywhere at Minzhu Lu

外地人去了户部巷就来到汉阳门
Outsiders come to Hanyang Gate once they've been to Hubu Xiang

车子多 人也多
All those cars, all those people

满街放的流行歌
With pop songs filling the streets

只有汉阳门的花园
It's only the garden at Hanyang Gate

还属于我们这些人
That still belongs to us

('Hanyangmen huayuan' by Feng Xiang)

If the constants of local life can become so prominent in the music capturing imaginations under exceptional historical circumstances, what of more common periods themselves? In 2014, I spent time in Wuhan investigating precisely the 'pop songs filling the streets' that in Feng Xiang's song align squarely with the encroaching world of 'outsiders' (*waidi ren*) and represent the antithesis of belonging. Untouched by the heightening effects of the crisis to come, the mood for collectivity I found expressed in this aspect of the city's musical life was naturally less palpable and more ambiguous. My focus was 'Passion Square' (*jiqing guangchang*) – a recurring kind of street music show embedded in a wider ecosystem of other public-space popular music sounds and practices, including street-side karaoke, recorded music played out from the thresholds of businesses and square dance exercise gatherings. Passion Square had spread as far as Hanyang Gate Garden itself, along with a handful of other spots in the city, in performances held every afternoon and evening. Going beyond representations of Wuhan in musical texts, this research offers a sight of the on-the-ground realities of collective musical experiences in the city, one that majors on more unassuming practices – in this case, primarily dependent on face-to-face modes – that are ubiquitous in mundane urban life (García Quiñones, Kassabian and Boschi 2016).

My main conceptual point of reference is community, a notion widely and consistently employed to summarise how people associate around musical practices and products.[1] It is a term of collective life considered unique in 'never being used unfavourably' (Williams, in Day 2006: 14), and the idealisation of 'communal' forms of living has been called an era-defining 'leit motif' of contemporary thinking (Gusfield 1975: 87). Discourses of community around Chinese-language popular culture – those noted and reinforced in scholarship – clearly resonate with singer Feng Xiang's nostalgic sentiments; Marc Moskowitz, for instance, finds 'urbanisation and the break-down of community' to have left many 'feeling isolated, lonely, and unsatisfied' – a central function of Chinese pop is apparently to provide an outlet for these negative feelings (Moskowitz 2010: 53). So, is community a useful term of reference for Passion Square? If so, in which aspects of the practices is it a meaningful construct and where do its limits and boundaries lie? Characteristics of Passion Square that I outline below – to do with embeddedness in public-space life, immediate physical situations, musical materials, modes of performing and audiencing and so on – make this a fitting case for looking beyond the 'ideal types of musical communities' represented by common discourse and theory in music studies and elsewhere (Torp 2017: 235). Central to my aim is recognising and countering the risks of overstating and idealising around musical community, complicating the notion in light of less neat realities found in more mundane experiences.

This task rests on growing attention paid to 'the active participatory role of social agents in the sensory production of sociality' (Harris 2020: 27). In this

---

[1] The concerns of this Element are distinct from those of 'Community Music', a field of participatory research and therapeutic intervention aimed at producing benefits for participants who are 'socially or culturally disadvantaged' (O'Grady and McFerran 2007: 15).

case study, emerging most pertinently from a focus on the sensory is what Adam Krims calls the 'geographical fact' of music-related activity and the meanings made through it (Krims 2007: xv). Krims describes, for instance, how the physical separation of a CD retailer's classical section from its other departments through features of the shop's design is a material manifestation of that genre's rarefied status. Accessing this level of meaning involves approaching both humans and non-human things as potential 'source of action' as they interrelate (Bates 2012: 372), a way of fleshing out precisely what lies behind the abstraction, 'the social' – associations between elements, be they human or not (Latour 1996: 369). A major theme, then, is the geographical facts of Passion Square – in a broad sense: how collectivity plays out on an immediate level in material circumstances, shaped by sonic interactions with wider city life, built on the cooperative construction and sharing of spaces. This focus is the key way in which I bring ideas of musical community into better dialogue with ambiguities of experience here.

A second way involves a subtle change of language. I turn away from the singular countable noun 'a community' or the plural 'communities'. These words are inextricable from the idea of entities or collections of people to which individuals can belong, enduring bodies defined by the duality of insiders and outsiders. Instead, I use the uncountable noun 'community', evoking a descriptive quality of a situation or strip of activity. I argue that it is more useful, in line with the complexity of lived experience – and less coloured by what I critique below as a quickness in typical discourses to valorise community – to acknowledge that facets meaningfully talked about with the language of community can come in and out of focus, ebb and flow, as various elements intersect. Ultimately, this reflects an intention to eschew the pursuit of this quality as a vindication and the corresponding implication that where it is diluted is a deficiency. Finding community is not a 'solution' in a search for meaning in musical experiences. But versions of the notion, I argue, can be a useful reference point when decoupled from idealising tendencies and when their foundations are scrutinised.

1.1 Passion Square

Filming from high up on the Great Yangtze River Bridge in Wuhan in 2014, I am looking down on Hanyang Gate Garden, the same small area of green space that would capture the imagination through Feng Xiang's song in virus-hit times six years later. This rather unkempt miniature park would be entirely unassuming were it not for its position beneath the historic bridge, set between the banks of China's great river and this city's most famous landmark, the Yellow Crane

Figure 1. A view of Hanyang Gate Garden from the Great Yangtze River Bridge, with one of its patios below and the Yellow Crane Tower in the distance (photo by the author, 15 May 2014)

Tower (Huanghe Lou) (Figure 1).[2] On the patio directly below, a woman in her thirties with microphone in hand steps towards a few men of more advanced years, all of whom are perched on plastic stools among the loose semi-circle of people gathered around her. As she sings, she stoops to extend a hand to several of these spectators in turn. The first shows no obvious response, staring unmoved at the singer for a second or two before allowing her to grasp his

---

[2] For a less nostalgic picture of Hanyang Gate Garden's relatively recent condition, see a news report by Hao, Wang and Yin (2005), which describes it as a 'blot on the landscape' (*dasha fengjing*), being 'occupied by mah-jong tables, small peddlers, unisex massage, and crowds of people going to the toilet wherever they please.'

Video Example 1. Passion Square performance in Hanyang Gate Garden, viewed from the Great Yangtze River Bridge (video by the author, 15 May 2014) Video available in online formats.

fingers for a perfunctory handshake. She tries again with another man and he instinctively withdraws his hand, first opting to placate her with a wave-cum-salute before he changes his mind and submits. One more is staring at the ground as she approaches and seems caught off guard as he returns her greeting. The woman resumes the centre of her patio 'stage' just as a shower of twenty or thirty small-denomination banknotes is tossed in her direction, a tip from another audience member designed to flutter to earth around her feet (see Video Example 1).[3]

It is impossible to tell from up here which classic or more recent Chinese-language pop hit she is singing – not because the music fails to reach us, but because its details are obscured in a cacophony of five other similar performances going on in parallel in the park. Some have live backing bands of keyboard, drums and saxophone or trumpet, while others play recorded accompaniment through smart-phones connected to the PA. Down below, however, each of the six stages seems to carve out a functioning niche in this challenging sonic environment, against the wider backdrop of the traffic and other sounds of city life all around them.

The hesitancy – perhaps even resistance – with which these men respond to the singer's efforts at interaction is characteristic of these Passion Square shows. The 'passion' here is not necessarily of a romantic or sexual kind but instead holds connotations of fervour and excitement – ironic, given the prevalence of moderate behaviour I witness. The 'square' refers to the feature of city design originally

---

[3] Special thanks are due to Petr Nuska for his indispensable video-editing work, skilfully helping to make the very best of the footage I shot in Wuhan.

associated with the mass rallies of more highly politicised times in China's socialist history, but now it is a more fluid term (Kendall 2019: 119) and it seems to matter little that there is significant variety in the kinds of public space that actually host the activities. Plus, reference to squares links the shows to the much better known phenomenon of *guangchang wu* (square dancing), in which older urban residents all over China exercise to dance beats (Seetoo and Zou 2016).

These singing sessions are held daily in a few clusters in central Wuhan, with crowds of dozens and sometimes over 100 gathering in derelict sites, street-corner locations and green spaces like this one. Most in the audiences are middle-aged and older men; many come especially for these shows and stay for their two- or three-hour duration. Some individuals present singers, who are almost all younger women, with cash tips during the singing – the primary way to express appreciation and solidarity (Video Example 2). This practice is part of a gift economy in which cycles of reciprocity carve out ongoing relationships between singers and a minority in their audiences who become patrons. Values reach impressive heights, many songs attracting several individual tips in multiples of 100 yuan (around 16 US dollars at the time of my visit) and, occasionally, they can go into the thousands (see Horlor 2019a) – these gifts afford Passion Square singers a comfortable living. But, more generally, people watch in an apparently impassive state and usually engage with one another and the musicians undemonstratively. During my initial visits, I am struck that no one around me taps a foot to the beat or is obviously stirred by the music and barely any spectators exchange more than a few words with their fellows. What

Video Example 2. Passion Square singer Sihong receiving a cash tip during a
performance in Hanyang Gate Garden (video by the author, 15 May 2014)
Video available in online formats.

Georgina Born calls an 'aggregation of experience' certainly occurs (Born 2013: 29); on the most basic level, audience members go to Passion Square prepared to be among people, aware that they all contribute. But first glance points to an ambivalence in the ways many embrace or submit to this aggregation – it is certainly something humbler than, for instance, the 'deindividuation' that may be felt by members of sporting crowds when they chant in a state of 'reduced self-awareness and concern for social evaluation' (Herrera 2018: 488).

During visits to Hanyang Gate Garden in the early stages of the first of two research trips in 2014 totalling four months in duration, I sometimes come across a regular audience member, a Mr Wang. In his forties and married, he splits his time between the family home back in his native Qingdao, 800 kilometres away on China's northern coast, and the base for his watch business here in this city of around 10 million people, the capital of Hubei province. When in Wuhan, Wang lives the life of a bachelor and we joke about the freedom of being far from his wife. The first time we meet, he leads me around several of the park stages, where he is clearly well-known; each one has up to fifteen singers who take it in turns with two or three songs on the microphone. Several approach us to offer cigarettes and bottles of iced tea and to exchange a few words. I have already heard Mr Wang talk about how his business has taken him to over forty countries, and today he looks to impress by mentioning that we have been chatting half in Chinese and half in English – in fact, his English barely covers a few words. We walk by close to the emcee of one of the groups; his job is to manage the rotation of singers and to orchestrate thanks to those giving tips, ideally chipping in with animated comments during the singing. Picking me out as an unusual presence at the shows, he greets me on microphone with a comical exclamation, acting as if lighting up with excitement at what my presence may imply: '*meiyuan!*' (US dollars).

The centrality of money for Passion Square singers is evident – in spite of some efforts to conceal it – as I subsequently get to know a few from each of about a dozen different shows. On stage, Yinzi and Longzi, identical twins in their early twenties, project a seamless persona that plays up a naïve innocence. They always dress in matching outfits and sing breezy tunes with a childlike quality – 'Yi ge mama de nüer' (A mother's daughter) or 'Nongjia de xiao nühai' (Little peasant girl) – conspicuous among the normal mix of ballads, rock anthems and up-tempo pop numbers. Unlike in many singers, who exude a genuine quality, I see a more ruthless approach beneath the twins' persona. Our conversations are dominated by descriptions of difficulties in their life; they talk about the poverty of their family left behind in Jingzhou, another city in Hubei province a few hours away and how shows often leave them in tears when their income does not match the generally enthusiastic reception for their singing. Indeed, the more vocal of the twins, Yinzi, avoids many of my questions about Passion Square, saying 'you will have to slowly understand' or similar – I start to see our conversations largely as bids for my pity. I eventually experiment with ways to make them open up, giving small cash tips a few times when they get together to perform a unison duet. While they ordinarily leave me largely alone as I watch the shows, as soon as I give any tip, they switch to a proactive attitude, coming over to spend time chatting and welcoming my questions. Perhaps my experience parallels those of typical audience members I see them fraternising with, men who may be drip-fed attention in exchange for their gifts. The wariness of many to engage with singers could be for fear of becoming entwined in these reciprocal dynamics.

Yinzi and Longzi's Passion Square stage is not among those here beneath the Yangtze Bridge, however. It is a couple of kilometres away in a larger riverside park, on the banks where the Yangtze meets its longest tributary, the Han. Instead of organisers setting up from scratch the PA system every day, a mat or box to act as a temporary stage, lighting, audience seating and canopies, here, Passion Square takes place on four semi-permanent stages, each consisting of an open-sided arena with roof, a raised stage with in situ PA, lighting and projector screens (Figure 2). Shows are held in the evening rather than the afternoon, audiences and gifts are larger and there is a more formal feel to the organisation. The stakes feel a lot higher here, too, so it is understandable that the twins take a serious approach to what they do. The same feeling also impinges on my experience as a spectator; the presence of comfortable seats in prime position at the front, one of which I am ushered into whenever I visit – a privilege of the special guest or major gift giver – marks these shows out from the apparently undifferentiated crowds in the more modest settings. I begin to feel the impact of shows' material circumstances in how I relate with other people present.

I get to know Passion Square singers by spending time with them away from shows. One day, I meet up with a relatively new acquaintance, A-jia, while she is in the chair at a hair salon. We then talk over lunch about her distant home province and the tough economic circumstances that pushed her to leave four or five years ago in search of a living made through singing. Like almost all the singers around Wuhan's events, her performing career is founded on an enthusiasm for music that originated in childhood, rather than on any formal training in music. Indeed, the humbleness of her education is apparent to me when she struggles to write in my notebook common Chinese characters found in the names of songs she sings – or perhaps this is more a symptom of a recent smartphone-dependent lifestyle. It was only a few months before that she chanced on the opportunity to come to Wuhan, but she has doubts about continuing with this hard and unstable way of life, naturally desiring a return to her husband and three-

Figure 2. Yinzi and Longzi's stage (photo by the author, 11 May 2014)

year-old son. Indeed, within weeks she is called back home as her husband and mother-in-law – herself unwell – are struggling to cope after the child injures his hand in an accident. Next, we browse a local shopping arcade for outfits she will wear on stage and A-jia talks me through the balance she tries to strike between dressing up (*daban*) and maintaining her preferred modesty. As we walk, I point her attention towards a political poster that, like hundreds put up all around Wuhan by the authorities, displays the 'Core Values of Socialism' (*Shehuizhuyi hexin jiazhi guan*) (Figure 3).[4] I wonder if she might feel inclined to talk about

---

[4] These values are: strength and prosperity (*fuqiang*), democracy (*minzhu*), civility (*wenming*), harmony (*hexie*), freedom (*ziyou*), equality (*pingdeng*), justice (*gongzheng*), rule of law (*fazhi*), patriotism (*aiguo*), dedication to work (*jingye*), integrity (*chengxin*) and friendship (*youyi*).

Figure 3. A typical public-space hoarding displaying the twelve 'Core Values of Socialism' (photo by the author, 22 December 2014)

her performing in light of the wider discourses saturating public space in the city, but she responds blankly: 'I hardly ever pay attention.'

1.2 Musical Community

If, then, my preoccupations when considering Passion Square do not always align with the concerns of the participants, does my interest in community translate at all more generally in this context? How does it fit with any conceptualisations of the activity that prevail around Passion Square, especially considering how these understandings might intersect with wider patterns in Chinese language? Indeed, do broader theorisations of musical community adequately take on board the nuances of vernacular terms and conceptualisations, variable as they may be in their overlaps with the English 'community' and in their degrees of pertinence in their individual contexts? *She* (社) is a 'hallowed concept in Chinese political thought', carrying connotations of grassroots communitarianism and community spirit across various ages in China's history (Rowe 1984: 249; 1989: 95). From this come various related words, not only *shehui* (society) – which, in turn, gives way to the *shehuizhuyi* (socialism) that is so prominent a term public life in Wuhan – but also a cluster whose meanings intersect with 'community' in English, one close match being *shequn* (Harris 2020: 24). On the microphone or in conversation, I find Passion Square participants to call on *she* mainly with reference to a further idea, *shequ*;

although this word can refer to a state of community (Xu 2008: 34), people here use it specifically to stress to me that their activity does not belong to the contemporary institutional realm of the *shequ* (literally a residential community or neighbourhood) and instead that it is organised in a private (*si*) one.

These nuances are a reminder that community is fundamentally a notion of the way aggregation of experience is understood subjectively; it should not be mistaken for part of an empirical reality or assumed to exist independently of people who recognise it (Gusfield 1975: 25). In this sense, it would seem theoretically essential to take the lead from participants' representations of a practice's collective character or indeed, in the case of Passion Square, to heed the growing picture of their indifference to such discussions. But if the attitudes of the singer A-jia and others hint that these ideas are not among the main conceptual reference points or factors motivating activity here, should community immediately be consigned to a position of irrelevance? An argument against comes in how stubborn a notion 'community' is in contemporary ethnomusicology. As an idea implicated in various scholarly agendas within and related to the discipline, its theoretical foundations demand continuing attention, as do the different kinds of work done in its name, alongside consideration for how it might be taken forward.

In work with members of the Karen ethnic group in Thailand, Benjamin Fairfield encapsulates a typical – perhaps normative – discourse about music and community: funeral songs 'played an integral role in building community through enjoyment, courtship, anticipation, and nostalgic reflection' (Fairfield 2019: 481). Likewise, Jennifer Post assesses a performance of a narrative song in the Kazakh diaspora in Mongolia as 'a collective expression of community solidarity focused on maintaining continuity with ancestral history, landscape, and the cultural expression that ties it together' (Post 2007: 61). If these examples hint at some of the common ideas with which community is linked in mainstream ethnomusicology, the notion most explicitly steers the field of applied ethnomusicology, being embedded in its very raison d'être: scholars here set out to make 'a music-centered intervention in a particular community, whose purpose is to benefit that community' (Titon and Pettan 2015: 4). The notion not only shapes conceptualisations of the 'who' of this work, but it is also part of the 'what' that its benefits are comprised of – a participatory action research initiative, for instance, might be framed as providing 'a platform for people to address issues of identity, meaning and community' (Impey 2002: 13). Similar language accompanies recent work interested in 'repatriating' collections of musical materials, framed in the positive as 'taking recordings from the archive into the community' (Landau 2012: 264). And 'community' also resonates strongly in the realm of cultural institutions;

most prominently, it is embedded in UNESCO's goals surrounding intangible cultural heritage (UNESCO 2018; see also Harris 2020: 49).

In the latter context especially, the notion has attracted some criticism for its part in enabling governmental actors to exploit the appeal of related ideas such as 'national community' while actually 'limiting independent local practice and harnessing cultural traditions to propaganda initiatives' (Harris 2020: 49–51). Academic uses of the notion have also received direct – but still isolated – criticism for involvement in idealising representations of certain musical practices. A notable voice is Helen O'Shea, who exposes a dissonance between contemporary researchers' 'up-to-date toolkits of self-reflexive methodologies and dialogic relationships with their collaborators' and the comfort they seem to find in building investigations from 'an imaginative cultural narrative that seeks wholeness and community' (O'Shea 2007: 18). Indeed, it is tempting to impose such a narrative – one of 'grassroots authenticity' – on Passion Square as a way of finding legitimacy in the practices and, by extension, personal validation in studying them. It may be even more so for situations where the emotive experiences of marginalised or persecuted groups are involved.

But what theoretical foundations lie beneath the common ways ideas of musical community have been harnessed? Most theoretical work tends to focus on self-consciously intensive or extensive collective engagements on bodily and affective levels (Clayton, Dueck and Leante 2013: 10) and on the fervent negotiation of identities, often marginalised ones and in online or diaspora settings (McGuire 2018; Harris 2020). In a contribution that has become the first point of reference for many subsequent scholars, Kay Kaufman Shelemay points to three kinds of identity on which these processes often focus: the first two are those of descent (related to religious, ethnic and social inheritances) and of dissent (involving shared opposition to a particular state of affairs) (Shelemay 2011: 367–73). A rich literature emerges, for instance, about Muslim populations finding solidarity in sound as religious identities interact with wider ideas of national citizenship in various territories (Lee 1999; Eisenberg 2013). Shelemay's third focus is identities based on affinity: shared allegiance to particular forms of cultural expression, such as musical genres (Shelemay 2011: 373–5). This idea joins several that highlight processes of belonging focused on musical forms, including 'interpretive community' (Lum 1996) and 'genre community' (Lena 2012).

Based on Benedict Anderson's famous notion of 'imagined community' (Anderson 1991), these versions of musical community predominantly look at groups of people for whom the notion itself has currency, where there is some degree of self-conscious reflection on, or pursuit of, community ideals. But the work deals less well with situations arguably more typical of the bulk of musical experiences in human life, ones where collective engagement and commitment to group expression are ostensibly muted, where the practices set out to be mainstream, inclusive and acceptable to most rather than to recruit a strongly committed few. Passion Square is an ideal case study through which to build on current approaches; mundane circumstances less accessible to notions of descent and dissent, and an apparently weaker sense of affinity shift focus from self-conscious ideologies of community towards collective engagement based on intersections among human and non-human elements.

1.3 Passion Square and Community

Passion Square's core repertory of music is the canon of Mandarin dialect pop classics from the 1980s onwards, some of the music with the most universal familiarity possible in this context, considering the modern ease of access to stylistic diversity. The mainstream reach of the music may generally speak more loudly to some demographic groups than others, but its relevance is certainly not limited to any recognised marginal population, underground movement, subculture or counter-public. Participants rarely express a strong commitment to the particular forms and activities on display, at least not on an active level; audience members I speak to at shows sometimes tell me they prefer other kinds of music, especially local opera genres. But they are clearly at least able to tolerate what is played here and, as I explain later, it suits organisers' profit orientations to dissolve boundaries around the kinds of people who participate, rather than to highlight potentially divisive identity issues involving demographically or politically orientated kinship. Larger unifying themes and concerns such as national identity are among the many that are touched on in the music, the content thematically diverse rather than clearly targeted at one particular concern or group (see section 6, List of Songs).

My usage of the phrase 'Passion Square' itself requires a caveat so as not to overstate how firmly any discrete identity for these practices is inscribed in language. While the phrase comes up in my one-to-one conversations with musicians and organisers, I rarely if ever hear it used on microphone at shows; instead, when performers address audiences publicly, they refer to the assemblages in general terms such as 'venue' (*changzi*), 'stand' (*tanzi*) or 'stage' (*wutai*), and they sometimes use the names of their individual stages.[5] It is well-established that the formalisation of distinct identities, on levels of both individual psychology (Pelczynski 1984) and broader culture (Gusfield 1975: 36), is highly dependent on recognition from outsiders – how a group is defined linguistically can reflect characteristics and exceptionalities identified externally as well as internally. But

---

[5] Stage names include Xingguang yanyi (Starlight Performing Arts), Jianghe da wutai (The Great Rivers Grand Stage), Wangjiang da wutai (River View Grand Stage), Lanxing da wutai (Blue Star Grand Stage), and Gaoyuan shidai da wutai (The Highland Era Grand Stage).

I do not find 'Passion Square' to have any wider currency beyond the people most actively involved; those I ask to introduce me to the events during my early stages of fieldwork, including audience members and staff in nearby businesses, usually use more general descriptions for what takes place, simply calling them 'amateur' (*yeyu*) performances or 'singing and dancing' (although dancing is never more than a minor part).

Indeed, I find little evidence that 'Passion Square' points more broadly to an established entity of any kind; unconnected people I know from Wuhan and elsewhere in China have little sense of the events I describe to them and even when I show video clips, they can only guess that the music must be part of wedding celebrations or similar one-offs (see Video Example 3 for a representative performance excerpt). Occasional mentions in local media only reinforce the idea that general public consciousness is unfamiliar with the practices; the gatherings are called 'grassroots stages' (*caogen wutai*) (China News Service 2014) and the performers 'grassroots artists' (*caogen yishujia*) (Yuan 2014), while equally general terms are used for the activity itself: *maiyi* or *maichang* (performing for a living, literally 'selling art' or 'selling singing') (Ju 2014).

In some senses, it may be intuitive to align Passion Square with typical discourses of community – particularly as they are apparently informal in their organisation and they bring people into mutual orientations with others from their immediate local area in sustained and repeated ways. But, on the surface, there are also several factors complicating this inclination. It is because rather than in spite of its complexities and ambivalences that Passion Square's

Video Example 3. Excerpt from a typical Passion Square performance, by singer A-jing in Hanyang Gate Garden (video by the author, 15 May 2014)
Video available in online formats.

collective dimensions demand to be taken seriously. The broad 'geographical facts' of the practices provide the main lens for exploring how qualities of collective experience emerge in the interaction of bodies, the combination of sounds and the construction of space.

1.4 Fieldwork

This Element emerges primarily from participant observation at over fifty Passion Square shows in the spring and autumn of 2014 – in a variety of different locations in Wuhan. While present at performances and other events, I straddled several roles. I participated in ways that were little different from other audience members, watching the performances from among the spectators. I interacted with fellow audience members and became one of the known individuals whom singers at different events would look out for, chat to and extend hospitality towards. While my questions and requests to performers like the twins Yinzi and Longzi sometimes made these exchanges quite different from those between other participants, I sensed that even for some performers who got to know me relatively well in my role as a researcher, I was still treated as a potential patron. Sometimes, this was framed as singers bestowing the favour of teaching me the customs of this unfamiliar social world in the hope of receiving my tips as a reward; but, in general, I gained a relatively representative experience of the kinds of discourse and mode of interaction that usually prevailed. I was wary of entering the gift-giving exchanges, attempting to balance active partici- pation with distance from relationships too overtly mediated by money. I repaid the openness of other contacts in different ways; one backing musician, for instance, asked me to sing several times at another kind of performance to which he contributed and despite my being a novice singer, involving a foreign visitor obviously reflected well on him. With others, I settled into the role of privileged outsider: I was taken into confidence about information from private lives not shared with peers, invited to sit 'backstage' at shows and told specifically by several singers that they did not expect tips from me. I was invited to numerous meals and various other occasions spent with performers on a one-to-one basis and as part of groups involving audience members and I also had online text chats with singers and backing musicians.

But while this broader ethnography led me in particular to deeper understandings of the gift economy (Horlor 2019a), and the overlap of everyday and performance realms (Horlor 2019b), the complications of community I have already outlined make it appropriate to call less on the representations of collective experience offered by Passion Square participants. Instead, my focus widens to the level of group behaviour, how people interact spatially and the materiality of these experiences. I consider Passion Square as a part of a wider ecosystem of sound in the city, conducting sound surveys of the public space of the central portion of Wuhan, covering – to the best of my knowledge – all the Passion Square events active at the time. I recorded the precise locations of any musical activity that I encountered at different times of day in a 3 km x 4.5 km area of the city's centre, ultimately focusing on two main categories alongside Passion Square: recorded music from businesses and square dancing. These observations give way to various senses in which aggregated experience here points to complications in musical community.

2 Acoustic Spaces

This Element, then, is about moving beyond community as tied to reflection on (symbolic) commonalities shared among people. In fact, tracing long-term development in notions of community points instead to significances in how people are differentiated from others. This is the idea I take forward to begin discussion of Passion Square's realities, highlighting in particular sound, embedded in broader material experience, as formative of differentiation – the first lens for exploring complexities of community here.

2.1 Beyond Symbolic Community

Since the late nineteenth century, 'the major framework within the poles of which sociologists have set their discussions of human associations and social changes' is the distinction between informally and bureaucratically organised collective activity (Gusfield 1975: 1) – in other words, between *Gemeinschaft* (community) and *Gesellschaft* (society) (Tönnies [1887] 2001). This framework has been used to account for living circumstances in their ongoing and comprehensive senses: a general level of differences between, for example, rural and urban lifestyles. Of lesser concern to this formulation seems to be narrower strips of collective activity isolated within bounded timeframes. The idea of *communitas*, by way of contrast, evokes a version of community involving fleeting and intense oneness, a bonding that transcends institutional structures and social groups, being neither 'rooted in the past [nor extending] into the future through language, law and custom' (Turner 1969: 113).

But not all group experiences have these transcendent qualities and recent scholarship has addressed a gap concerning more commonplace aggregation of experience, one that nonetheless is rooted in shared activity more than organisational or ideological commonality. The idea of 'communities of practice' points to mutual engagement, joint enterprise and shared repertoires found in a range of assemblages, from those pursuing a hobby together, to groups of employees and even families (Wenger 1998). And the ensuing idea of 'communities of musical practice' (Kenny 2016) explores characteristics that are of obvious relevance to Passion Square, especially the idea that people can belong simultaneously, with different degrees, to multiple communities of practice and that these communities rarely have clear self-designation strategies. But the idea also puts emphasis on collective learning and improvement, something not immediately reconcilable with Passion Square, where joint goals or measures of progress are not evoked specifically.

Increasingly, however, research seeks to decouple this focus on mutual orientation from the self-consciousness with which mechanisms such as cooperative music learning are employed to foster belonging, by instead highlighting the embodied and sensory sides of these activities. Scholarship on soundscapes, for instance, has been drawing connections between sonic experience and community from its very beginnings. Building on the famous work of R. Murray Schafer (1977), Barry Truax terms 'soundmarks' those sounds that are important in fostering 'acoustic community' (Truax [1984] 2001: 66) – they carry a unique significance for a certain group of people, so act as the primary means by which the group recognises and defines itself. A compelling example is residents living near to an airport united in their suffering from aircraft sound disturbance (Schafer 1977: 214). There are now well-established reservations about some of the starting points from which these ideas emerge (Parmar 2019: 5), particularly the refrain that a 'deterioration' of sonic conditions since the Industrial Revolution has caused a modern excess of sounds: '[T]here is so much acoustic information that little of it can emerge with clarity' (Schafer 1977: 71). But if this work finds ideal manifestations of acoustic community in rural and past forms of living, a branch of more recent work, while still optimistic about sound's contribution to community, is more accepting of the hubbub of contemporary life. There are calls for the 'community established and maintained by acoustic communication' to be shaped into 'a reliable, healthy, and resilient' one (Titon 2015: 23). For Brandon LaBelle, this kind of community does not reject sonic markers of modernity or noise; instead he proposes that noise 'might act as a form of deviation that, in circulating through neighbourhoods, can fully aid in the emergence of community' (LaBelle 2010: 84).

In doing so, LaBelle touches on an important aspect of theory about community overlooked in some accounts about music (for example, Wang 2003: 150) – the role of hostility and conflict. Drawing on early twentieth-century theorist Georg Simmel, William Rowe's social history of nineteenth-century Wuhan argues that the notion of community carries stronger meaning in this city than most others in China. This is the result of certain demographic and geographic conditions: 'systematic bonds of antagonism and competition' held together the contemporary city's three districts (Wuchang, Hanyang and Hankou), which were separate towns until the twentieth century (Rowe 1989: 206). That people view outsiders with hostility (as opposed to indifference) contributes clarity to group boundaries and builds a sense of belonging to larger wholes, raising a consciousness of different parties' stake in one another's existence. This counters the sense that 'individualistic' urban lifestyles are antithetical to community; instead, it is argued that the division of labour, recognised in such contexts by Émile Durkheim, breeds mutual dependence (Durkheim [1893] 1960). If ideas of community come back to the differentiation of people, then this is most vivid in contexts of heterogeneity, rather than in past living circumstances of resemblance and traditional kinship.

Taken further in another direction, however, these ideas start to complicate the faith that typical discourses of community place in its connection to benevolent fellow feeling. Differentiation and the building of belonging necessarily involve both 'a positive identification with the "we-self" and a negative distinction from an "other" through border drawing' (Fairfield 2019: 471). And the idea of community does not rule out dependence on the less appealing processes of discriminating and disparaging (Ramnarine 2011: 331), even in their extreme forms; Ross Cole, for instance, draws connections between Edwardian English folk song theorists' motivating notion of 'racial community' and ideologies of fascism (Cole 2019: 36). To absorb positive discourses of community, holding the notion up as an ideal, without sufficient consideration of its counterpart exclusion, is not only to turn a blind eye to all that is possible to say and do in its name, but also to imply alignment with past forms of living and music in their supposedly local, traditional and spontaneous qualities.

2.2 Differentiation

Back in Hanyang Gate Garden, a man near me clumsily bumps the arm of another spectator's plastic garden chair as he moves a stool into place to watch the performance. The seated man reacts angrily, making an aggressive gesture as the other continues to position himself nearby. This small incident has disproportionately angered the seated man and, realising his error, the other apologises, gives up on placing his stool and, instead, takes it to the other side of the audience circle to sit down. Singers tell me that in Passion Square there are 'no real friends'; for them, audience contacts are only customers (*keren*) and fellow performers are competitors whose conversations with me they sometimes actively disrupt and about whom they talk badly to me (Horlor 2019a: 23–4).

Video Example 4. A performance by singer Wenwen, with the sounds of other stages in Hanyang Gate Garden becoming audible as the song ends and the microphone changes hands (video by the author, 17 May 2014)
Video available in online formats.

After an hour or two in the park, I feel a little dazed. The air is saturated with cigarette smoke and with electronic cymbals crashing over nasal vocals. I have to cup my hand to Mr Wang's ear to continue our conversation and passers-by and off-stage singers use their fingers as earplugs when they move too close to the speakers. I gesture that I need respite and retreat a few steps from immersion in this group's sonic sphere. As I withdraw, the current song gets consumed by other sounds that it had previously masked – the music of the next nearest group, the generator powering the session and the road nearby, all of which ordinarily only come into perception when the singing pauses for the microphone to change hands (Video Example 4). The placing of the event's speakers traces the shape of the audience group, encircling us all in this sphere of sound. The equipment is old, however, and it periodically cuts out for a few seconds before someone manipulates a loose connection back to life. When there is light rain, organisers prop open umbrellas over the electrical equipment, only cancelling shows on very wet days. Feedback screams out as off-stage singers absent-mindedly move too close to a speaker with a microphone in hand.

In the features of Passion Square I describe here, there is evidence that, to at least some degree, people involved acknowledge stakes in one another's existence. Sound, in particular, is worth dwelling on as a territory of differentiation in aggregated experience at Passion Square. I do so inspired by research with a similar interest in public-space music and the acoustic conditions of the contemporary urban environment: Paul Kendall's study of the social space of

Kaili, a small city in China's southwest. Kendall casts 'amateur' music making as a casualty of the modern concentration of leisure practices into 'high-decibel environment[s]', with unamplified sounds driven out of public spaces such as squares and into hidden indoor settings (Kendall 2019: 69). His focus is the kinds of musical practice surrounded by rhetoric overlapping considerably with community discourses, that of a 'cultural authenticity' (*yuanshengtai*) based on localness, self-organisation and tradition (Kendall 2019: 92; see also Rees 2016: 74). Passion Square groups, in spite of the precariousness of their technology, thrive in these high-decibel public spaces – an uncomfortable fit with this version of cultural authenticity. In 2014, I find them in about half a dozen corners of public territory in Wuhan's central areas and, notably, almost every stage is part of a cluster with between one and five others. Their arrangements initially strike me as counterintuitive, putting shows in such proximity that it is hard to identify visually where one audience ends and the other begins and the cacophonous sonic environments seem far from ideal (Kendall 2019: 21). But rather than passing over amplified practices like these as irrelevant to authenticity, community and related ideas, a closer look at their sonic interactions – the roles of sound in how groups occupy and share these spaces – points to the differentiation that brings them instructively into these conversations.

Figure 4 represents the positioning of two Passion Square groups in a small city square. This is the kind of proximity I initially think of as unhelpful for the functioning of a musical performance, with it apparently unavoidable for each

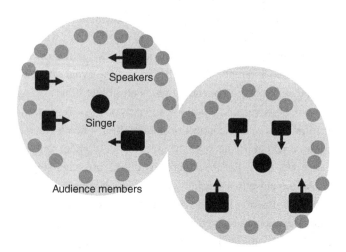

Figure 4. Bird's eye view illustration showing the positioning of two Passion Square groups and the diffusion of sound from their respective sound systems (not to precise scale)

one's sound to interfere with that of the other. But as I spend more time in audience circles, I realise that their proximity actually plays a role in encouraging people to be immersed in one or the other. The direction and loudness with which they emit their sounds allows the two groups to operate well together, with each set of participants absorbed in a sphere dominated by their own group's sounds; music that is potentially disturbing to one set is masked by that group's own. By taking just a few steps outside the primary dissemination zone of one stage's sound, the effect is lost; the sounds of the other creep back in and create cacophony. The stages enjoy a highly effective acoustic independence from each other, in spite of their physical proximity and a group-level interlocking of experience emerges – groups as well as individuals share stakes in one another's existence.

The directional emission of sound establishes difference and allows boundaries to be experienced. To function, Passion Square stages rely on carving out spaces within a sound environment that threatens the flow of the activities, forging aggregations whose primary commonality is their shared isolation from potential disturbances through sound masking. But if 'sound explicitly brings bodies together' (LaBelle 2010: xxiv), for Jeff Todd Titon, Erving Goffman's notion of 'co-presence' provides a reminder that community relies not only on people being near to one another, but that they engage with one another, that they communicate (Titon 2015: 29). From the proximity here, perhaps co-presence emerges in what has been called 'orientational behaviour' (Kendon 1990: 212). How people position and direct their bodies in concert with others creates spaces over which they 'maintain joint jurisdiction and control' (Kendon 1990: 211) – a small group in a conversation, for instance, usually claims the space between its participants, making it unlikely to be encroached on by others as long as that orientational layout persists. The loudness of the music at Passion Square means that people coming into the range in which one group dominates over others are very likely to orientate themselves in concert with other people there, contributing to the circle of bodies that works together to bring a show into being, to turn someone merely singing into someone performing on a recognisable stage. The sonic conditions make it virtually obligatory for people in proximity to invest at least some attention in one group over another, so that together they produce a social occasion from the undifferentiated public street.

Acoustic space is talked about as 'a sphere without fixed boundaries[. . .] not a pictorial space, boxed in, but dynamic, always in flux, creating its own dimensions moment by moment' (Carpenter and McLuhan, in LaBelle 2010: xxi–xxii). But while the boundaries of a sphere like this are characterised by philosophers as ambiguous or imperceptible (Born 2013: 13), in the parks, squares and streets of Wuhan, the sphere of each stage is, in fact, 'boxed in' by those of others and they function to orientate people precisely because the limits are well defined. In this sense, these are acoustic spaces with private qualities nesting within a wider public one, akin to when individuals block out sounds they cannot control by listening to music through headphones (Born 2013: 26).

While, however, the leakage of headphone sound to those outside is minimal, when I film from high up on the bridge overlooking the park or retreat from the immediacy of a sphere, the cluster of stages starts to operate as one in projecting its cacophony into the city. This has consequences that are both detrimental and beneficial for their ends. On one hand, while I am in Wuhan in 2014, almost all of the Passion Square stages I know come under pressure from the authorities to relocate to places where they will not cause noise disturbance to residents (Ju 2014). On the other, the cacophonous sound of a cluster alerts people over a large area to a lively happening. *Re'nao* (literally 'heat and noise') is a highly desirable phenomenon in Chinese contexts (Chau 2008), and the word comes up frequently in my conversations about the appeal of Passion Square (Horlor 2019c: 48). Indeed, there may be further culturally specific factors; the American leader of a university a cappella group in China comments to Kendall on members' remarkable ability to create 'a personal acoustic space' by filtering out sounds of others rehearsing around them: 'given the high-decibel levels of the[...] soundscape, perhaps this [is] a necessary talent to acquire' in urban China (Kendall 2019: 161).

What causes an aggregation of experience around Passion Square is the emergence of a bounded performance through the orientation of people in concert, these people primarily differentiated from a wider public through sonic means. It is significant that Passion Square shows almost always find a home in freely accessible public spaces rather than legally private ones where access is controlled. As can be extrapolated from Michael Warner's (2002) theorising on publicness, public-space music is like other forms of expression in recruiting a specific kind of audience; its locations, timings and practices specify to some extent the kinds of people that generally participate in or hear it. In streets and similar places open to all, however, as well as its core audience, this music potentially reaches thousands of people who receive it unwittingly or reluctantly. Ordinary public territories play host to a mixture of classes, ages, genders and lifestyles and their music is, in many cases, no more than a background to a range of other activities. In contrast to many musical contexts in which collective experience is explored – including those in everyday life where music is secondary to other things – this music is not ambiguously indexed to a particular task or action among people with pre-existing relation-ships. This distils the sense in which the physical arrangement of bodies is not just part of a group identity here, but it is, in fact, the very crux of a common (albeit precarious and fleeting) awareness.

Titon raises a useful parallel with ecosystem ecology, especially involving the non-human world, where the concept of community points to 'the interactions among populations of different species inhabiting a given area' (Titon 2015: 35). This notion of community comprises both competitive and cooperative behaviour among and between species. Just as the aggregation of experience at Passion Square is founded on co-presence and orientational beháviour with the input of sound, the community among non-human populations looks beyond reflection on ideals of belonging. In Wuhan's parks and streets, distinctions between insiders and outsiders, and between the public and the private, play out in material dealings involving space and sound. Groups negotiate coexistence among themselves to manage potential conflict and to raise the possibility of a concerted agency. But whereas Titon sees similar processes in 'peak music-making experiences, when the music seems to be making you rather than the reverse' (Titon 2015: 31), the phenomena I identify around Passion Square do not require unusually heightened feeling or intensive engagement. If there are peaks in musical experiences, the inevitable flat moments and troughs also deserve attention as part of what it means to engage musically. Resisting the compulsion to call either the group of people around one show or the larger cluster 'a community' as an enduring and self-reflexive entity, attention can turn towards the emergence of a quality of community in the aggregation of experience. The concept is useful here for pointing to the material processes of differentiation in public life and it is this level of analysis that seems well suited to the many moments making up non-peak musical experiences.

2.3 Complicating Community: Sharing Spaces

It is worth briefly revisiting the connection some scholars of Chinese music have drawn between urbanisation and the weakening of community. Although contemporary research on modern Chinese musical practices is largely attuned positively to what is afforded by urbanness (for example Stock 2002), work that specifically tackles community and the city can sometimes start from more nostalgic perspectives. Stephen Jones, for instance, is an outspoken advocate of the 'values of local communities', at times directly contrasting them with 'modern metropolitan culture' (Jones 2013: 26). Urban living continues to expand in China and, with this, people with heterogeneous identities and concerns are increasingly concentrated into proximity within small areas of territory. It is the concentrated heterogeneity characteristic of publicness that amplifies potential for conflict and disagreement. In an example from further afield, Andrew Eisenberg analyses an incident reported in the Kenyan media in 2006, in which an expatriate living in Mombasa is frustrated by being woken up each morning by a local mosque's call to prayer. When she complains to the mosque's imam, there is a dispute during which she is physically assaulted. Eisenberg sees the incident as illustration of the potential for people to understand public space differently. The foreign resident assumes it to be 'ostensibly neutral', so considers the call to prayer an unacceptable intrusion; while, for the imam, the sacredness of the sound secures its precedence over other concerns. The crucial idea I take from this episode is of the ontological dispute at its heart, the potential for public space to be understood in conflicting ways (Eisenberg 2013: 197).

This potential supports rather than undermines qualities of community emerging as a useful description of the aggregation of experience in Wuhan. The competing interests, and even ontologies, of events and local residents, citizens and authorities, and between different music groups, do not indicate remoteness of community. Instead, they are at the heart of differentiating people – audience members emerge from the general public all around and boundaries are drawn between different groups involved in an activity. People here are often in close physical proximity to others, so the processes that differentiate people and produce meaningful co-presence are important. Musicians deal with these challenges not by seeking to distance themselves from other sources of loud sound, by moving their activities to empty spaces. Instead, they create pockets of territory towards which important sounds are focused, allowing participants to carry on their activity undisturbed by those around them. These niches mean that the activity can be meaningfully enjoyed and that groups can co-exist with others emitting similarly loud sounds. Rather than seeking physical separation, establishing sonic spheres of co-presence becomes a solution in the congested acoustic environment. This is not a harmonious acoustic public space in which co-existence is comfortable, but one in which disturbance, conflict and contestation are a fact of life. The space is not defined by restriction, but by a variety in sound and practice.

In an everyday context, where debate surrounding overarching identity issues of ethnicity, religion and politics is less prominent, life is instead dominated by these intimate-scale, mundane co-existence strategies, whose meanings pertain primarily to the personal and small-group realm. Considering spatiality, materiality and sound illustrate that group unity need not only be equated with rationalised identity issues. Collections of people define the boundaries of their group not only on an ideological level, but also practically, including through manipulating their environment. Although the loud music may create the conditions of noise arousal and fatigue that are among those linked to deindividuated states and *communitas* (Herrera 2018: 488), it is hard to imagine Passion Square's musical material being associated with any transcendent experience of this kind or with the breakdown of hierarchies. It is important to stress again my choice of language to talk about these issues. I do not see all those involved in Passion Square as 'a community' – instead, I consider their spatial and orientational behaviour as displaying some degree of community as a quality. This detaches the notion from the idealism of the grassroots and traditional, but it acknowledges that there is still a meaningful sense in which aggregation of experience occurs here.

3 Performance Layouts

As I leave an evening session, I bump into a singer called Sihong. She is clearly frustrated as I ask how that evening's takings have been – business is not good. Her park group has recently been banned (*qudi*) by local police from performing outside beneath the Yangtze Bridge and they have instead been forced indoors to a previously deserted building alongside the river promenade. She complains that there is not as much passing trade (*liudongxing*) here, even though the sound still spills out onto the street and curious people may move freely among the three stages that share the building. It is not only that the park shows are too loud (Kendall 2019: 114–18), but Sihong suspects their monetised nature to be part of the problem for the authorities; she is incredulous that a couple of street-side karaoke stands nearby, with customers paying to sing a few songs, are still allowed to go on as normal.

A Passion Square event might easily be confused for a karaoke session, at least until it becomes clear that singers at the former get paid rather than pay for the pleasure. Although in Wuhan, as in other locations across China and beyond, karaoke takes place mainly behind closed doors in commercial Karaoke Television (KTV) centres, a few stalls pop up each night on street corners. They draw small crowds of passers-by who might stay to sing two or three songs having paid 10 yuan to the organisers. Earlier in the evening, I spend a few minutes at one of the karaoke stands that perturb Sihong. A young woman in front of me is obviously excited about the chance to sing, but she also seems scared by the prospect, collapsing into nervous laughter with her boyfriend and imploring him for reassurance before finally resolving to hand her money to the organiser.

The activity is arranged – deliberately or not – in a way that seems encouraging and supportive to reluctant performers like this. The singer sits or stands several metres away, facing the video screen and speakers, which project the song back towards them. The singer's attention is fixed on the screen and other

Figure 5. A street-side karaoke gathering, with the singer and karaoke
screen both circled (photo by the author, 20 May 2014)

participants take up positions in a rough semi-circle not opposite them, but
around them, allowing as many people as possible to stand at the singer's side,
all bodies orientated together towards the video screen (Figure 5). The physical
layout is not a typically adversarial concert set-up but something that might be
called more 'participatory' (Turino 2008); here the singer temporarily takes on
a specialist role, but one barely reflected in a largely undifferentiated arrangement of bodies.

As detailed above, the forging of acoustic spaces can comment on community
as a quality in the aggregation of experience in Passion Square. But once
established, are there different kinds of acoustic space? Can one, for instance,
be made 'more collective' by the character of encounters enabled by the
arrangement of human and non-human bodies, as in the karaoke example
(Kendall 2019: 162)? Sally Harrison-Pepper maps various forms of activity in
New York City's Washington Square Park – including jogging, chess and
various forms of music making – in relation to the physical features of the
park (Harrison-Pepper [1990] 2010: 55). People here display habitual pathways
in their uses of the square, in their routes and interactions with its street
performers. For Harrison-Pepper, a 'spontaneous "communitas" emerges' as
a result of the park's layout, the diagonal walkways channelling visitors towards
street performers and encouraging intensive personal interaction (Harrison-
Pepper [1990] 2010: 64).

But this interpretation does not fully account for the distinction between
proximity and co-presence; the qualities of interaction between people cannot

necessarily be read in the potentials that material layouts may afford. Likewise, the weaker differentiation in how the bodies of people playing different roles are arranged at the karaoke stand in Wuhan, rather than pointing to solidarity and strong collective identification, might perhaps simply be a manifestation of context-specific approaches to performing. In other environments, such as bars in the United States, karaoke is portrayed as an opportunity for singers briefly to imagine themselves as superstars (Zhou and Tarocco 2007: 36). But different conceptualisations seem to guide the activity here; a slogan plastered on the equipment of one group reads: 'Music makes you healthy and happy! Let's all sing together to our heart's content!' (see also Mitsui and Hosokawa 1998: 17). Making a spectacle of oneself is apparently not a necessary part of performing in public in Wuhan; I find echoes among musicians playing for leisure in parks in the city, many of whom turn their bodies to face walls or otherwise position themselves out of clear sight, even though they invariably use amplification equipment and direct this towards a potential audience.

3.1 Qualities of Interaction in Passion Square Venues

What are the connections between Passion Square's material circumstances and qualities of interaction in the continuing complication of community discourses? There is significant variety in the material layout of shows across the city. Some groups set up rudimentary equipment in derelict corners, while a few others perform in the well-equipped arenas I introduced earlier. Among the more modest settings is a space close to the foot of Jianghan Bridge, a road crossing spanning Wuhan's second major river, the Han. The group operating in this location has been forced to adapt to a programme of demolition and renewal that has slowly changed the landscape of their corner of the city over the course of several years. They initially occupied a relatively wide, if unremarkable stretch of footpath beneath a slip road rising towards the bridge proper. Since I first found this Passion Square stage in 2012, however, the space has constantly evolved; several blocks of wholesale business premises and residences that once lined the street have been demolished and new development has gradually emerged in place. When I return in October 2014, work has already begun to reshape the footpath and the construction site is bounded by a new temporary wall, set further back from the road. Now, the group is squeezed in between the wall behind and the road in front (Figure 6). Organisers suspend red cloth between the trunks of trees lining the road and this functions as a screen to seclude the event from the traffic.

In all of the iterations I witness, the group and its audience – which consistently peaks in the region of a hundred people – squeeze into rubble-

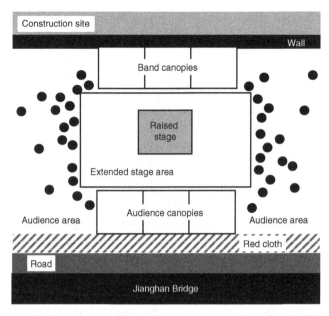

Figure 6. Bird's eye view plan of the arena near to Jianghan Bridge, as of
October 2014 (not drawn to precise scale)

strewn and unusually shaped spaces. Performers and audience are largely
unable to assemble according to the traditional theatrical arrangement in
which the two groups are counterpoised facing one another (Schafer 1977:
116–17). Instead, the layout more resembles a 'thrust-stage', with the
performer surrounded on three sides by the audience. Along similar lines
to the connections Harrison-Pepper makes between movement around the
built environment and qualities of interaction, this form of theatrical archi-
tecture is sometimes associated with efforts to promote 'warm human
exchange' between performers and audience (Tuan 1982: 13). In this case,
the unusual shape of the available space forces most of the audience to
gather not in front of the stage but to its left and right. A man moves
towards the stage from the left side while a singer, A-jing, is facing towards
the audience on the right. He comes from outside her field of vision and she
remains oblivious to his presence for a few moments. The giver stands
awkwardly with cash outstretched but cannot make himself noticed.
Eventually, another singer who is crossing the arena close to the stage
directs A-jing's attention to the man and the gift is finally delivered.
Under ideal circumstances, a singer would make efforts to extend the
duration of the interaction with her benefactor, holding courteous eye
contact as the man approaches, bowing in thanks as he hands over the

cash and offering a few words of gratitude timed to fit between lines of melody. Public recognition is an important driver of the money-giving practices in Passion Square (Horlor 2019a: 22–4), but features of the layout compromise this singer's ability to engage with her patron.

On other occasions, singers exploit the space to produce remarkable consequences in the character of interaction. Among performers at this event, and indeed throughout each of Wuhan's shows, I find stage behaviour almost always to be highly reserved. Singers usually stand in a fixed position in the centre of the stage, barely moving off the spot and showing few signs of bodily engagement with the music. One performer from Henan province, Ximei, combines a rendition of the song 'Shei shi wo de lang' (Who will be my man) with a lively – and rather raunchy – dance. Soon after the song starts, Ximei jumps down from the raised stage onto the extended stage area at ground level surrounding it, dancing all around the arena and approaching all sections of the crowd. At various places, she falls into exaggerated sexualised poses and the audience is sparked into an unprecedented flurry of positive responses. In keeping with the ethos of the events, this general animation is quickly expressed in the most tangible of forms when dozens of spectators begin offering cash gifts. Instead of waiting on stage for givers to approach and deliver the money, Ximei actively circulates around the arena to collect it. People compete to be the next to gain her attention, waving bank notes in the air. Soon, a member of the organising team begins following her as she dances to all four corners, holding out a bucket to be filled with money.

The singularity of Ximei's act is undoubtedly amplified by her identifying as transgender. Bouts of spontaneous laughter arise when she sits down on the lap of a man in the front row and the emcee jokes of introducing a new charge of 100 yuan per sit. Later this man gives her a cash gift and the audience is delighted again when Ximei kisses him on the cheek. The emcee whips the crowd into a relative frenzy, exclaiming excitedly and breaking into laughter each time the dancer enters another suggestive posture. Women in the audience clap, smile and offer money and an unparalleled number of smart phones is held up to film the show. The extended stage area around the main raised section usually functions as a buffer between performer and audience, perhaps dampening the intensity of their interaction. When Ximei breaks away from the normal patterns in the use of the space, the result is unprecedented engagement and a palpable sense of excitement. Richard Schechner formulates the street performance audience as an 'eruption', with those in the heated centre showing the strongest engagement (Schechner 1988: 159). A cooler rim spreads from this central point towards the periphery and the people in the most distant parts are the least engaged, perhaps even primarily focused on some other concern or activity. At the end of Ximei's song, a groan rises from the audience and around half of those present immediately stand up to leave. The performer exploits to great effect the spatial possibilities of this setting in a way that contributes to the difference between a commonplace performance and a remarkable one. When I see Ximei perform in different locations, her offerings are far more standard in their content and in the responses they engender.

Accounts of transgender performance in Chinese contexts have highlighted the real erotic potency that can be conjured up (Wu 2004). But perhaps considering the highly public nature of Ximei's dance in Wuhan, it is not surprising that eroticism gives way to humour and a novelty appeal. She arrived in Wuhan months before, after a spell working in nightlife venues in another provincial capital. The organiser of the first Passion Square event Ximei performed at following this move helps me put in context the performances I witness. The stage organiser is convinced that the unusual audience reactions I see do not result from a particular appreciation of her performance, but from the audience's enjoyment of a curious (*xiqi*) spectacle. After a similar initial impact, the receptions Ximei achieved at this organiser's event quickly settled down as spectators began to treat this singer as any other and the former is convinced that the novelty will eventually wear off at the event near Jianghan Bridge, too. Novelty, she tells me, is a key tool for new Passion Square performers or events seeking to establish an audience, but simply good singing is enough to support the relationships with individuals on which a successful performing career is sustained thereafter. Occasionally I witness singers around Wuhan adding variety to their offerings by showcasing other skills, such as playing musical instruments or performing various kinds of dance. One, Ganzi, tells me that by offering belly dance performances, she is proactively attempting to compensate for lesser singing success. I never see any of the more unusual performances make an impact similar to Ximei's, however.

It is possible to see community as a quality of the mutual physiological engagement of bodies with music. Combining empirical measures with ethnographic insight has encouraged some to stress coordinated movement's meaning in the aggregation of experience, most effectively again in contexts where belonging is a well-defined topic of reflection and a goal of interaction. In Afro-Brazilian village Congado rituals, for instance, the spiritual power of a percussion and dance collective is demonstrated through its ability to maintain in-group synchronisation rather than falling into line with other ensembles encountered during processions; there is a musical and ritual 'imperative to resist entrainment whenever groups belonging to different communities meet during the ritual' (Lucas, Clayton and Leante 2011: 75–6). The 'collective effervescence' that followers of Durkheim might read into Ximei's performance is a one-off (Clayton 2013: 33), extraordinary against the standard of static and moderate behaviour and not reflected on or idealised in the same way. But this episode does point to the significance of other goals that participants bring into Passion Square arenas. Money is both the key motivating factor for performers' activities and also the primary sign of interpersonal engagement. This issue connects Passion Square with another facet of typical pictures of community, one concerning collective orientations.

I have noted that the absence of explicit collective aims, such as those found in musical learning, undermines Passion's Square's alignment with ideas around communities of musical practice. Instead, the centrality of economic motivations has further implications for complicating common discourses. Community is associated with highly interdependent lives and shared goals, while isolation and self-interest represent its antithesis. Segregation and orientation to the self is supposedly characteristic of the contemporary city. Often this interpretation attaches a negative judgement to urban living (Freie 1998), although Durkheimian notions of 'organic solidarity' emerging from mutual dependence on the division of labour in industrial societies set up a strong counterargument (Durkheim [1893] 1960).

The gift-giving practices, and their foundations in one-to-one contact between singers and audience members, might be interpreted as lending Passion Square a fundamentally individualistic character (Horlor 2019a). Key evidence comes in the on-microphone rhetoric of emcees, where the individual benefits of participation are emphasised over any form of group solidarity. People giving cash are often thanked by name at the end of a song and good wishes are offered for health and prosperity (Horlor 2019a: 15). During the winter, singers and emcees redouble these rhetorical efforts. The groups that continue throughout the year's coldest months adapt by preparing their spaces differently, attaching thickly padded curtains to their overhead canopies and frames, effectively enclosing participants in walled arenas. Bodies are encouraged into closer proximity and expressions of gratitude and admiration abound for those hardy individuals showing such commitment to attending. This dedication becomes a focus to justify plying these potential money givers with hot drinks, singers gaining capital from a battle with the elements, an excuse to bombard customers with the hospitality calculated to inspire reciprocal gifts. As I explore later, these individual goals are motivated not by warm interaction for its own sake, but by the instrumentality of interpersonal interaction in the extraction of money.

Chinese societies, those found in various territories of Asia and in diaspora contexts worldwide, have typically been categorised by sociologists and psychologists as showing strong collectivistic inclinations. These orientations are often explained as expressing the legacies of Confucian thought (King 1985). But some scholarship scrutinising the translation of doctrine into real-life activity rejects the notions of individualism and collectivism as meaningful in the Chinese context, proposing tradition and ritual as alternative pillars (Stockman 2000). This work raises a distinction between in-group and out-group relationships; interaction with strangers and wider society is supposed to be indifferent or hostile in Chinese societies, while among family members and close friends, people are highly committed to others and focused on group rather than personal goals. The matter is complicated still further in light of ethnographic research, in which observation of altruistic and selfless behaviour among Chinese people acting in public life does not seem to support these theories of out-group hostility. Perhaps Chinese public life even reflects 'civic community' (Jankowiak 1993: 164).

Real behaviour, then, does not fit neat distinctions between collective and individual orientations. Certain music scholarship, too, recognises that collectivism and individualism interrelate meaningfully. John Chernoff, for instance, describes community as the 'forum within which individualism is realised' in the context of African drum idioms, noting that communities 'build ethnic solidarity and cohesion from individualism rather than conformity' (Chernoff 1979: 162). This might even be framed as evidence of the unusual potency of musical experiences in these processes, considering 'the individual and personal benefits that may accrue through the increased sense of belonging to a collective that musical interactions seem capable of bringing' (Clayton 2017: 219).

Indeed, in Passion Square, the pursuit of individual goals is enabled not by social and sonic isolation, but by actors embracing the aggregation of experience. An equally notable dimension of profit orientation is the strong ethos of inclusivity that organisers are encouraged to promote. As I have noted, an essential part of the shows is music that is widely accessible, a repertory familiar and acceptable to most rather than a focal point of strong identification for the few. As well as its forms and symbolic contents, however, the music's acoustic properties also play a role in generating a potentially heterogeneous public. Not only does this popular idiom have the amplified sonic footprint that allows for the spread of the *re'nao* cacophony into the wider city (Horlor 2019c: 48–50), but the loudness of the music within a group's sonic sphere suits quick exchanges with singers who are constantly circulating, rather than sustained conversation among groups of strangers who find themselves assembled closely and statically. The key theme arises again: community is a quality most meaningfully found in the differentiation of people. As connected to the identity work done symbolically by music, Passion Square's money orientations breed inclusivity rather than discrimination. But other qualities of aggregation, following the differentiation of people, do emerge in further ways, again requiring a close consideration of spatial-material factors.

3.2 Differentiating Status

At this evening's show, A-jia surprises the audience by accompanying herself on the drums as she sings the song 'Zhu ni ping'an' (Wishing you well). The novelty of this skill is surely calculated to reap extraordinary financial rewards, but, in fact, it receives absolutely no cash gifts, a scenario virtually unheard of for any song at Passion Square. A-jia's stage is in the same cluster of four on which the twins Yinzi and Longzi sing every night. With their fixed stages, semi-permanent structures, and relatively advanced technology, these arenas represent a development on typical Passion Square shows in various ways. But A-jia has not accounted for the unique layout of this stage actually hindering the flow of gifts. The drum kit and accompanying guitarist are placed on an elevated gantry to one side of the stage and the audience has no established means of delivering their gifts up there to A-jia. When she comes down to the stage for the next song, the money starts flowing again as normal. In general in this arena, though, gift giving is not the inclusive practice it is elsewhere. Instead of the audience member having personal contact with the singer while delivering cash, money is more often thrown onto the stage from the wings or handed to a member of the organising team to pass on. At most other events, sizeable tips punctuate a steady flow of smaller gifts whose values are within reach of the average audience member. Here, though, only a few gifts occur during each song, but almost all are of several hundred yuan and they are given by a smaller group of individuals who enjoy recognisably higher status.

In Kendall's part of urban China, the rhetoric attached to notions of the 'culturally authentic' (*yuanshengtai*) places this phenomenon in 'the square and not the theatre' and defines its practices as 'self-entertainment and not performance' (Kendall 2019: 92). This cluster of four materially advanced stages highlights the complexities in Passion Square's relationship with these two interconnected binaries exposed by Kendall's research and by extension with community discourses. The binaries speak to Thomas Turino's opposing ideal types, 'presentational' and 'participatory' performance (Turino 2008). In the former, musicians are specialists and there are clear distinctions between their active roles and the passivity of those confined to spectating. The latter kind of performance is associated with communal music making in which the production of sound is a collective responsibility. Passion Square's migration, from the city square to, if not the theatre, then a layout recalling certain characteristics of this setting, intersects with ideas of community in their entwinement with issues about interpersonal dealings, economic patterns and genre.

With its musical repertory dependent on canonical pop records, it is tempting to align Passion Square with broad ideas of popular music's individual presentational qualities, perhaps in contrast to a typically participatory idea of folk – the centrality of money intuitively chimes with this reading. But the types of economic exchange in Passion Square are quite different from the formally structured arrangements underlying mainstream popular music, characterised as a model of 'indirect patronage' (Booth and Kuhn 1990). In Wuhan's parks, squares and streets, support is not anonymised and intermediated as it is represented in this model. Gifts are ideally delivered to the musician in a face-to-face manner and these personal acts colour subsequent interactions between giver and beneficiary. They are tied up in the complexities of the dealings between people known to one another on an individual basis, involving the history of their contact, the balance of reciprocal obligation that currently exists between them and what effect on the relationship a gift might produce (Horlor 2019a). In some senses, this reflects the 'direct patronage' most associated with the history of Western art music, where major support from single donors enabled musicians to sustain careers (Booth and Kuhn 1990). But rather than relying on a particular wealthy individual, street musicians juggle personal relationships with many of these direct supporters. And while the patronage involves direct contact between two parties, it also depends on the intermediary of the organiser to whom the singer hands their takings for it to be redistributed again at the end of the session, minus a cut. This covers the costs of organising and supplying the facilities and it provides a profit incentive for stage bosses. In Marxist terms, the presence of this middleman points to the production of surplus value and completes the process of the 'commodification' of the music (Taylor 2007: 282).

The instinct to draw boundaries between popular and folk practices has, of course, been thoroughly problematised by generations of scholars (Revill 2005). Likewise, Turino's ideal types of presentation and participation are not intended to fully describe real practices. But these ideas are useful insofar as they help approach the meaningfulness of the arrangement of bodies. In African performance contexts, Karin Barber (1997) finds differentiation of seating and position within an arena significant as expression of social status. Likewise, in keeping with the more exclusive gift-giving practices at this cluster of Passion Square stages, audiences here include a small proportion of relatively high-status individuals: local entrepreneurs, media and arts managers and sometimes perhaps even government officials. Unlike derelict or street-corner sites, this setting befits socialising, impressing others through conspicuous generosity and intimacy with singers and developing connections. A slightly more complex map of the arena emerges, in which social hierarchies are expressed in the specific positions within the space that particular social groups occupy. Typically at Passion Square events, the scope for singers to acknowledge and convey respect for an audience member's status is limited to their interpersonal interaction and the exchange of gifts. But here, those with a track record of generosity or otherwise closely connected with the singers can also be ushered to a special section along one side of the arena. Whereas in the ordinary audience enclosure, spectators simply stand or perch on plastic stools, here a limited number of comfortable chairs are grouped around tables. The tables nearest to the front receive the most consistent attention and hospitality from the performers and this is where the highest status individuals are accommodated.

It is worth emphasising that part of meaning found in the gift economy comes in being recognised in one's gift giving by other people (Horlor 2019a); the spatial-material differentiation of status is a key mechanism here. Again, this is a matter of the differentiation of people enabling a recognition of how they relate to one another, encouraging them to see their stake in one another's existence and to cooperatively construct an aggregation of experience – becoming a co-present audience through awareness of its construction. This points to qualities of community not based on likeness (as in the ideas of descent, dissent and affinity), but on difference. More broadly, it emphasises that spatial-material operators are the stuff of how experience aggregates. Interactions between participants are enabled and constrained by the layout, ambient conditions and acoustic environment found at events, partly constructed through the positioning of bodies and by the emission of sound. Space within Passion Square's sonic spheres is carved up and made socially meaningful, enabling people's experiences to interlock through their differentiation.

4 Performance and Society

Kendall notes the significances in urban China's everyday musical life of 'conceived branded space', referring to the ways in which people's experience of their environment intertwines with official representations of the city (Kendall 2019: 32). Like Kaili, his case-study city, Wuhan has its own repertory of local messages; prominent during my time there in 2014 are the phrase 'the Wuhan spirit' (*Wuhan jingshen*) and various references to the idea of Wuhan as a river city. These messages join a collection of more generic political slogans, especially the 'Core Values of Socialism' and the 'Chinese Dream' (*Zhongguo meng*) as an almost constant presence in the city's public life. Beside the content of these messages, however, their positioning in the built environment now brings Passion Square into

Figure 7. Public-space poster featuring riverside scenes of Wuhan, attached to a temporary fence around a square under refurbishment
(photo by the author, 20 October 2014)

dialogue with issues of collective organisation, control and authority, extending the complication of community discourses in their politicised dimensions.

The messages exert a direct influence on the acoustic public space of the city; spoken forms of rhetoric are broadcast out into the street by police vehicles on the move, by speakers at school gates and by the PA systems in public transport and supermarkets. Smaller shops and other facilities with scrolling display boards or video screens intersperse their own content with visual versions of these official slogans, just as they are found on bus stop advertisements, outdoor hoardings, subway promotional spaces, street furniture and other kinds of poster and screen. Home to some of the most extensive of these messages are the temporary walls and fences erected around building sites, derelict areas or other places to which general access is restricted (Kendall 2019: 62) (Figure 7).

It is precisely this kind of space that provides typical locations for Passion Square performances. Openings are established in walls or breaches made in fences to allow participants access to these restricted sites, so spaces that in the day time are left deserted by the will of the authorities are redefined by the presence of music groups to become viable places for leisure activity during evening hours (Figure 8).

(a)

(b)

Figure 8. The city square cordoned off by temporary fencing, deserted
by day (above) and hosting a Passion Square show in the evening (below)
(photos by the author, 20 October 2014 and 27 October 2014)

In the context of Kendall's study, amplified music is considered the antithesis of a typically rural phenomenon, 'self-organized amateur activity that
occurs as a natural expression of everyday life[...] for the sake of self-

entertainment' (Kendall 2019: 92). Recorded music piped into urban public spaces by authorities and businesses is contrasted with the 'traditional' practices of members of minority ethnic groups. If the latter is an ideal manifestation of the community (*Gemeinschaft*) realm of organisation – spontaneous and informal activity based on affectual ties, intimate knowledge and the intrinsic value of human relationships – amplified musical practices, particularly those featuring a pop idiom, might easily be consigned to the social (*Gesellschaft*) realm of institutional and government structures, with relationships deliberately fostered to achieve rational goals in an emotionally neutral way, often involving prescribed duties in the dealings between ranks (Tönnies [1887] 2001; Day 2006).

I come across in Wuhan's public spaces plenty of galas and talent competitions organised by and with government authorities, entertaining while transmitting political and social messages (Figure 9). But Passion Square, along with streetside karaoke sessions, busking, square-dance groups, and small collections of musicians practising is organised without direct affiliation to formal commerce or state bureaucracy. Passion Square stages are run as petty businesses, with organisers providing the equipment in exchange for a cut of 20 or 30 percent of singers' tips and accompanying musicians, emcees and helpers handed a small flat cash

Figure 9. A dance contest on Wuhan's riverbank. Behind the performers is advertising for a state bank's credit card and on the sides of the stage are banners displaying the 'Core Values of Socialism' and Wuhan city branding (photo by the author, 25 October 2014)

sum at the end of each session. Promotion depends entirely on word of mouth and the projection of the *re'nao* cacophony into the city streets and recruitment of singers extensively harnesses family and friendship ties.

How, then, can these practices be interpreted in light of community discourses that place weight on qualities of organisation? If part of what 'community' implies here is an intermediate territory of free organisation and debate located between the individual and the state (Pelczynski 1984: 11), so, too, do two other notions that have been long-running themes for discussion among historians and social theorists studying urban China: civil society and the public sphere. Particularly debated is whether these terms, emerging from work by Hegel in the nineteenth century and developed by Habermas (1989), are relevant to Chinese societies. Perhaps their dependence on the presence of a literate bourgeoisie and the concurrent conceptualisation of a distinct private realm make them most suited to seventeenth- and eighteenth-century Europe (Wakeman 1993). There are, however, close equivalences between ideas of publicness and the Chinese term *gong* (公). The connotations of both have evolved in a complex manner over history, at various times being associated with government authority, involved in distinctions with the private realm or being synonymous with collectivity and communality (Rowe 1989, 1990).

Direct state influence over leisure has dramatically reduced in China since the first few decades of communist rule. Sport, recreation and cultural clubs have been blossoming since major reforms to government economic and civil policy in the late 1970s (Shue 1995). This activity might be described in similar terms to those George Revill applies to the diversity of music making occurring in England's provincial towns and countryside; he characterises a population 'participating in and interpreting [...] event[s] in a way which suit[s] their own ends in terms of a set of values distinct from those imposed from outside' (Revill 2005: 697). Indeed, in sound studies, heterogeneity in an urban environment's sound has been taken as evidence of varied social practices, a phenomenon equated directly with the qualities of community (Kreutzfeld 2010). By the same token, Kendall notes that China's liberalisation, and particularly the proliferation of motorised road traffic sounds accompanying economic development, has had structuring consequences in a spatial sense: '[L]eisure activity could no longer just happen anywhere but had to be ushered into designated spaces' (Kendall 2019: 61). As I explained earlier, Passion Square depends on forging functioning acoustic spaces within its clusters to liberate itself from this kind of restriction. But its commandeering of officially cordoned-off spaces raises the prospect of these processes proactively challenging the predominance of the 'social' realm of organisation. Moving into these spaces reconfigures, at least temporarily, definitions imposed on them by authorities – with the added symbolic significance of breaching the political branding that fortifies them.

But behind this prospect is the need for proper examination of the binary distinction separating community and society. In the context of Cuba, Geoff Baker scrutinises common discourses regarding the censorship of musicians, and binaries involving 'underground' and 'commercial' musics (Baker 2012). He concludes that underground musicians have greater freedom than is often assumed and that they even enjoy degrees of state support: '[C]ritics of the Cuban government tend to see censorship everywhere and to overstate the power and the limiting function of the state in the field of culture' (Baker 2011: 3). Far from rejecting their music being commercialised, underground artists explore various ways of generating income that blur the boundaries between official and informal realms. Likewise, Kendall talks about a temptation to imagine a duality of official and unofficial culture in Kaili. But this is also undermined by conversation with city residents, who, rather than either endorsing or rejecting official images of their city, are 'dismissive of both official and everyday music making within the city limits' (Kendall 2019: 15).

Kendall finds independent musical groups in Kaili prepared to move around to overcome the closing off of public spaces to their activities, and his conclusions fit the situation I find in Wuhan extremely well: '[I]it would be a profound misrepresentation to celebrate the relocation of music groups as tactics of resistance, given that groups were principally motivated by practicalities, as they grasped opportunities to create musical spaces wherever they could' (Kendall 2019: 127). Political engagement is not apparent in the ethos of Passion Square, and I find little evidence that participants reflect significantly on this side of what they do. Performance events moving into cordoned-off spaces might at most reflect apathy or disregard for official intentions; just like for A-jia earlier, who told me of her indifference to the branding of Wuhan's public space, these attitudes seem dormant until official policies interfere with everyday music making. A few individuals describe their activity to me as *minjian* (among the people; folk), a generic categorisation significant for the unofficial and unstructured connotations associated in various contexts of Chinese music (Lau 1991: 48). But is this evidence that participants attach ideological value to the nonprofessional organisation of their activity? The term is invariably used in a self-deprecating way rather than one communicating pride or claiming legitimacy. In keeping with other scholars' observations in China (for example Jones 2013: 28), use of the label *minjian* seems best understood as a humble acknowledgement of a perceived lack of sophistication and of an unworthiness to be called 'professional'. This humility is worth emulating, too, in any conclusions over Passion Square's alignment with communal over societal qualities in the organisation of aggregated experience.

More than this, though, the very prospect Kendall raises of 'celebrating' tactics of resistance only reinforces my commitment to decoupling community from idealistic instincts here. In his investigation of the sounds of Islam in Middle Eastern cities, Charles Hirschkind deconstructs discourses of purity in self-organisation. With particular reference to Warner's interpretation of 'publicness' (Warner 2002), Hirschkind calls the autonomy implied here a 'fiction', arguing that it 'builds in a structural blindness to the material conditions of the discourses it produces and circulates, as well as to the pragmatics of its speech forms: the genres, stylistic elements, citational resources, gestural codes, and so on that make a discourse intelligible to specific people inhabiting certain conditions of knowledge and learning' (Hirschkind 2006: 106). As well as through direct intervention, governmental and institutional impact is also felt in influences shaping the modes and conventions of expression by which people communicate in situations such as street performance. They are in no way isolated from the concerns and structures of wider society.

Although a public or community involved in musical activity may appear entirely independent, its functioning is underpinned by basic commonalities allowing participants to share an understanding of their circumstances and to engage with each other. Not least, Passion Square relies on a popular music vocabulary brought into people's experience through its bureaucratic production processes and regulated mass-media dissemination. More fundamentally, on-microphone elements of Passion Square are almost entirely conducted in Mandarin, even though, in behind-the-scenes conversations between insiders and spectators, the Wuhan dialect is widely spoken. Shared reliance on Mandarin and the simplified set of written Chinese characters (*jiantizi*) prevails not simply as the result of an 'organic' evolution, but due to the deliberate efforts of the government over the last sixty-five years. Indeed, Wuhan's public spaces still contain information posters encouraging citizens to speak in Mandarin (Figure 10).

Hirschkind's approach seriously destabilises the community–society axis; real activity does not live up to these ideal types. One illustration is found in the 'gift economy', how I characterise money exchange at Passion Square – the language deliberately calls to mind the 'instrumental relationships' of *guanxi* in wider Chinese life. Through *guanxi*, the rigidity of institutional society is penetrated by interpersonal dealings, as people harness sense of obligation

Figure 10. Poster encouraging the use of Mandarin
(photo by the author, 25 October 2014)

with the gifts and favours they offer to people well placed within institutional structures to repay them (Yang 1994). Human relationships, interpersonal obligations and morality permeate all kinds of scenario in which interaction between people is involved, not only grassroots ones. The societal or institutional realm is not remote from the connections, favours, bribes and interpersonal dynamics that this discourse of community equates inflexibly to less official areas of life. In Passion Square, the individual and instrumental sides of events' money-exchange practices feed off and enable meaning intrinsic to the relations between people. On the other extreme, too, a pure and disinterested picture of communal life is equally problematic and theoretical simplifications of this kind fail to reflect the complexity of real-world situations. Street music events do not exist in a community bubble, fully isolated from the dynamics of institutional society. In fact, the two poles of this discourse are not separate but intertwined.

On first glance, then, Passion Square might easily be characterised as expression of the will of real people overcoming bureaucratic organisation. Shows see residents making meaningful interventions into local activity, reflecting the bottom-up organisation that epitomises the *Gemeinschaft* version of community. By the same token, this alignment is complicated by their money orientation, presentational qualities and amplification, particularly when considered against wider discourses, including those around the cultural authenticity of *yuanshengtai*. Indeed, that authorities still retain the indisputable power to move on or to silence Passion Square points clearly to the limits of public space's 'democratisation'. But even were this not the case, the theoretical complexities that this situation exposes ultimately quell the urge to valorise marginalised actors apparently punching above their weight against hegemonic forces. Again, recasting community as a quality rather than as an entity means transcending the imperative to align a situation or aggregation with one ideal type or the other. And the ebbing and flowing of societal and communal qualities plays out in associations involving human and non-human elements. Indeed, sound returns as an important phenomenon when considering how 'power' is manifest in the intergroup relations binding Passion Square to the wider city.

4.1 Passion Square and the City

The singer Ganzi gives me a call in the afternoon to ask me to come a little early to tonight's Passion Square show; she wants me to help translate the English writing on the labels of some cosmetic samples she has acquired. Arriving at the square about fifteen minutes before the performance normally begins to differentiate itself from other public activity here, I am surprised to find the space occupied by a small band of acoustic-electric guitars and a saxophone. As I approach, someone attached to the group hands me a flyer and asks if I am a Christian. Meanwhile, the Passion Square sound system starts to fire up with a few bursts of a disco record, apparently as a test. But this act equally functions as a hostile signal; by the time my five-minute conversation to help Ganzi is over, I look around and find no sign of the Christian musicians. The vastly superior sound system of the Passion Square stage has cleansed the sonic environment and left questions of territorial ownership in no doubt.

Kendall emphasises that a consideration of social space means paying attention to its 'imbuement with time' (Kendall 2019: 105). Some formulations use this to go still further down the route of marking communal resistance to the social realm; he considers Michel De Certeau's distinction between the spatial strategies of governments and businesses, which have the power to define their own spaces, and the temporal tactics left to individuals and groups, who can only exploit the times when they might function within others' territories (Kendall 2019: 126–7). The binary language here might not be the most flexible, but it does begin to approach the interconnectedness of what are posited as two realms: space and time. Keeping in mind my reluctance to overplay the antagonism between local culture and institutional structure, the part of De Certeau's formulation I take forward is the idea that temporality intersects with discourses that have so far focused mainly on space; in Wuhan, sound is a mechanism of power in the intimate and mundane scale of relations between groups in the temporally dynamic soundscape.

A premise in early sound studies work is that producing loud sounds can express power, reflecting the sound maker's confidence that they will not be censored (Schafer 1977: 76). Comparing the proliferation of sound technologies in contemporary urban life with the more limited tools available in past centuries, Truax calls the modern access to loudspeakers a 'democratisation' of acoustic power (Truax [1984] 2001: 127). With this kind of equipment, ordinary citizens are now able to affect great numbers of people, a privilege only open to large institutions and authorities in the past. But, as hinted at when the Passion Square stage takes over 'ownership' of the area from the Christian band, this power to define a space is shaped into temporal patterns. Indeed, Passion Square is part of a spatial-temporal picture of mundane negotiation and co-existence, a wider ecosystem of musical leisure and other features of the general soundscape. Square dances are another notable player and their clustering is influenced by a particular series of spatial-temporal constraints partly imposed by the recordings emitted by shops and other businesses.

Like Passion Square performances, square dance groups' primary requirement is an area of ground flat and large enough to accommodate their activity. The city's widest boulevards, with their expansive footpaths, are inevitably already claimed by the general bustle of city life and filled with both road and pedestrian traffic. Indeed, many of the spaces that would otherwise be most suitable for square dancing are the same as those occupied by the shops and stalls that discharge loud music to attract customers. Streets that are physically suitable are made inappropriate for dances by the nature of the existing activity within them. There is, however, a solution to this inconvenience, in the form of a significant area of the city centre taken up by the Hanzheng Street wholesale

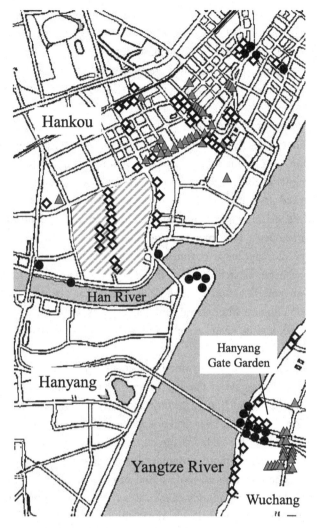

● = Passion Square stage
▲ = business emitting recorded music
◇ = square dance group
▨ = Hanzheng Street wholesale market

Figure 11. An approximately 3 km x 4.5 km section of central Wuhan
showing sources of public-space music. Based on map © OpenStreetMap
contributors, with data available under the Open Database Licence

market. The market is contained within a border of larger roads and these end up
being among the spaces in Wuhan most densely filled with square dance groups
(Figure 11). Not only are their footpaths of ample width, but, by the evening, the
market's intense activity has already calmed to leave them in a virtually deserted

state rarely found elsewhere in the city, with its spread of shops and stalls operating longer hours. By the evening leisure window, starting at about 7pm, there is almost no road or foot traffic on these streets and there are no restaurants or retailers emitting loud music – just business staff packing up for the night. These streets provide the perfect location, both physically and socially, for the dancers.

It is easy to see how processes that depend on reflection and ideologies of belonging (such as descent, dissent and affinity) might persist in time; belonging to communities becomes part of people's identities, it spills broadly into life beyond moments of musical behaviour by shaping their dealings with people who are marked as fellows or foes partly through musical activity. Musical practices of 'a community' might be enshrined in more enduring written discourses or be open at any time through online platforms – ideal-type versions of community may apparently be timeless. But how far do community qualities of Passion Square persist in time, given my interpretation that these qualities are forged through material co-presence more than reflection? In other words, how far does Passion Square, through the experiences of its participants unbound by ideologies of belonging, shape people's dealings with the wider city, perhaps through ideas of place?

There is little evidence that symbolic aspects of space have a particularly strong impact on the scale of the city overall. I once hear a performance of 'Huanghe Lou', a song celebrating the city landmark not far from Hanyang Gate Garden, the Yellow Crane Tower. But this is the only instance, from all of my observation at shows, of local themes featuring explicitly in the musical repertory chosen. In fact, it is more common to hear songs about geographically distant places; one common example is the song 'Tian lu' (Heavenly road), whose lyrics celebrate the building of the railway line crossing the plateaus of Tibet. The appeal of Passion Square's music and of the overall performance is founded on themes and modes of expression that resonate on a pan-Chinese rather than purely a local level. Again, then, place is not a factor overloaded with ideological significance and sense of place is rarely a major element of the meaning shared overtly at the events through the music or any other discourse.

Ruth Finnegan addresses the connection between 'local' practices and the sense of wider place, in the UK town of Milton Keynes. For the amateur musicians here, 'the concept of Milton Keynes as a *whole* [was not] of direct concern to most people in the everyday conduct of their musical (or other) activities' (Finnegan 1989: 300; emphasis in the original). This is a major factor in her decision not to class the town itself as 'a community'. Finnegan also explores the idea that local musical activity can reveal the presence of micro-level community within this wider context, considering how larger urban areas might be comprised of numerous smaller local units to which people feel strongly aligned – in other words, that the city is an 'agglomeration of village communities' (Finnegan 1989: 299). Ultimately, Finnegan concludes that the size, heterogeneity and complexity of Milton Keynes renders this model less valuable in that context. But qualities of micro-community might comment on the experience of a particular small group of singers in Wuhan, those whose stay in the city is relatively short and forms but a single station in a varied performing career.

During the day I spend at the salon, restaurant and shopping arcade with the singer A-jia, I come to realise that her life in Wuhan takes place in a very limited physical space and that it revolves around a social life almost entirely centred on the contacts made at Passion Square. Half expecting to move away when circumstances present a better living elsewhere, immersion in a sense of Wuhan as a place is in no way a prerequisite for performing success. A-jia is living in a modest hotel not far from her group's stage, unable or unwilling to invest in the deposit required to secure an apartment. Her daily life is conducted in the space of just a few streets surrounding this accommodation. In the context of the city as a whole, it is a tiny corner. These streets contain the restaurants in which she entertains her fans or customers during the daytime, the internet cafes in which she downloads the backing tracks for her performances and the salons and fashion markets she frequents to maintain her onstage image. As I get to know A-jia, I am surprised by her limited knowledge of Wuhan's geography. In spite of, for instance, browsing for stage outfits being a common use of her time, she is not aware that one of the city's main shopping districts lies close by, barely outside her local territory. While intensely invested in the shows and while the performances shape almost all aspects of her life, A-jia seems connected to the social life of the wider city to an unusually low degree.

In a sense, then, her experience has some of the character of the geographically and socially bounded scenario of an idealised (rural) community, although it takes place against the backdrop of a much larger and more heterogeneous potential social canvass. Parallels occur elsewhere in Chinese music culture; the DJs that Anouska Komlosy finds working in the western province of Yunnan, for example, mainly hail from Guangdong, more than 1,000 kilometres away. They are forced by their employers to share motel rooms, making for 'a very close, almost familial working atmosphere as the company members ate and lived together, in a way reminiscent of Chinese cultural performance troupes of the past' (Komlosy 2008: 62). But in A-jia's case, even one's local place within the city is a corner shared not only with known individuals but also with thousands of strangers engaged there for a huge variety of purposes. Here, the notion of one's local place exclusively as 'an area of common living' (Turner 1969: 96) is not a sufficient description and the qualities of this version of community are complicated in its participants' experiences, even from this wider perspective on Passion Square and the city.

Passion Square's meanings between people are enabled by a strong orientation to space as navigated with the senses, while also showing an indifference to a symbolic or politicised representation of place. The aggregation of experience is most meaningful in the association of people and material phenomena; sonic spheres help to differentiate participants and passers-by and spatial-material hierarchies distinguish patrons from peripheral players. But qualities of community are hard to pinpoint in ways that endure when these conditions cease. Again, approaching community as a quality rather than as an entity deals well with this divergence; it is not a solid fact of collective experience, but a quality that can colour aggregation, just as it can ebb away. In a model of de-idealised community not communities, this is not a failure but a reflection of the complexities of real experience.

5 Complicating Community

Although sometimes taken for granted, bringing the notion of community into a central position highlights its connections within a rich constellation of ideas. Common discourses evoked – and sometimes underlined – in music and wider scholarship depend on ideal types including localness, ruralness, the marginalised, *Gemeinschaft*, tradition, collective orientation, the acoustic, folk, participation, self-entertainment and the city square. These reference points are useful when establishing contrasts with agents and phenomena – perhaps governments or urbanisation – that more readily align with the other end of relevant binaries. But Passion Square simultaneously resonates with some elements associated with community in these various constructions, while also reflecting elements far less easily squared with the concept. Community does not stand out as an unambiguously pertinent notion here, particularly since it is not high on the list of concerns for participants. Understanding the aggregation of experience can still benefit from this reference point and my approach is drawn together by the decision to recast community as a quality rather than an entity. This helps detach it from the imperative of defining and naming groups of people, a process that can bring with it validating instincts and bind scholars into holding up community as a destination for their analyses. De-idealising community is about complicating conceptual pairs, it is at the heart of a model that finds legitimacy not in identifying clear boundaries but in recognising the interdependence of the apparently antithetical in real practices.

5.1 Beyond Binaries

Byron Dueck examines how face-to-face and imagined modes of sociability combine to bring meaning to musical experiences (Dueck 2007, 2013). His key notion is publicness, which he places on a conceptual plane that also includes intimacy. On the one hand, intimate sociability is contact with others on a face-to-face level, with people addressing one another based on their individual identities. Publicly orientated sociability and expression, on the other hand, mean 'mass-mediated forms of relating', those assuming an audience that potentially includes strangers (Dueck 2013: 13). Dueck describes the public and the intimate as 'intersecting modes of sociability that have come increasingly to constitute one another' (Dueck 2007: 56) as musical activity is facilitated by their interplay. Intimate encounters are enabled by orientation to generalised public influences and references; learning materials, musical customs and shared references can be harnessed by musicians as shortcuts to musical intimacy. Contact on an intimate level, too, can develop people's imaginaries of themselves as part of wider aggregations; face-to-face engagements through music develop materials, practices and forms of expression on which people can build a sense of larger scale belonging.

Similar mutually constitutive modes are found in analysis of various issues in Chinese musical life. Nimrod Baranovitch, for example, labels as 'symbiosis' the mutual reliance of potentially dissenting popular musicians and the Chinese state (Baranovitch 2003: 227). While dualities of hegemony and locality and state and society dominate discussions of this relationship, a closer look sees the two parties relying on one another for achieving commercial and ideological goals. A similar phenomenon entwines music industry structures with the practices of music listeners; artists and producers, for instance, respond to their work being assimilated into karaoke by including high numbers of slow songs on pop albums, aware that popularity is affected by karaoke singers' preferences for tracks that are easier to sing (Moskowitz 2010: 11). Indeed, in contexts such as karaoke, patterns of behaviour involving music contribute to social norms in a more general sense, too. Avron Boretz examines asymmetrical gender interactions in Taiwanese karaoke contexts, concluding that this interpersonal behaviour 'establishes and amplifies both individual identities within cohorts, and the hierarchical structure and behavioural norms of the cohort itself' (Boretz 2004: 194). Public space can be an arena for similar processes according to Florence Graezer, who notes that the practices of amateur dance groups 'establish a pattern and a rhythm to the social and cultural life of a locality by proposing and sometimes imposing norms and values governing everyday life' (Graezer 2004: 76).

Many of the binaries evoked by community discourses may be reconfigured as invitations to explore how individual experience, intimate interaction and micro-level association relate to macro-level phenomena of publicly orientated collective practices and expression. If in the broadest terms, the former level is the intuitive territory of community and the latter is its antithesis, then here I associate the experience of Passion Square with neither one clearly and instead demonstrate that both are indispensable to the wider picture. Mutual constitution, synergy and multiplicity offer a way of reconciling features that on first glance might seem inconsistent or contradictory.

5.2 Beyond Ideologies

Martin Stokes has argued that 'music is socially meaningful not entirely but largely because it provides means by which people recognise identities and places, and the boundaries which separate them' (Stokes 1994: 5). This Element is geared specifically towards aggregation of experience not accounted for by direct reflection on these identities and boundaries. Underlying commonalities play a part in bringing participants together and enabling meaning to circulate. One obvious factor that space constraints have prevented me from elaborating here is gender (see Horlor 2019a); with almost all singers being women and most members audience being men, this is clearly part of how people in different roles relate, choose the language they use to refer to each other, and exchange gifts. Interpersonal contact is clearly shaped by the identities that participants bring to the events and the meanings exchanged through participation stem from the common ground from which those involved approach the activities. But these commonalities are not thrust into the foreground as focal points to promote a sense of belonging, neither are they used to exclude any particular kinds of people. Rather, it is in the interests of organisers and performers to minimise the sense of distinction between insiders and outsiders, with one of the consequences being that affinity towards the musical material is felt only weakly.

Nonetheless, as Dueck puts it, participation in musical activity involves an aggregation of experience in the sense that people 'behave in ways that take into account the others around them, whether this involves getting to know them, moving with and around them on the dance floor, or keeping them politely out of frame' (Dueck 2013: 7). When people come together, they negotiate relationships with one another not only when they engage actively, but also when attending to the most mundane and basic necessities of inhabiting a shared space. Here, an ethos of inclusivity in musical and social terms brings people into contact with one another, fostering mutual engagement on a variety of levels and allowing them to display heterogeneous involvements in the aggregation of experience.

Clues are contained within the use of space, material and sound as to the events' relationship with community, for instance in how conflict and the sharing of space is managed and in the balance between institutional and grassroots definitions of public life and public space. Through encouraging bodies into proximity, these features are linked to orientational behaviour that fosters meaningful co-presence and the differentiation of statuses within a collection of people – in other words, making a group emerge fleetingly out of an undifferentiated public. The association of human and non-human elements is the very stuff through which the aggregation of experience plays out, the environment not simply the setting for social life, but the mechanisms through which it comes into being.

5.3 Beyond the Extraordinary

Musical activity can help to foster the connections between people, allowing groups to draw attention to themselves in public spaces, to attract likeminded people to their cause, and to develop a sense of what unites them. Groups can use sound and music to withdraw from others, to create, reconfigure or reinforce physical and social boundaries. The study of public-space music, then, seems particularly urgent when those involved have strong agendas for change, subversion, the radical transformation of identities or the escape from repression. Significant ethnic, religious, linguistic or political tensions are of lesser pertinence in the public life of Wuhan – but its streets, parks and derelict spots are arenas for conflict on a more intimate level. Passion Square performances exude a mundane quality, manifest not only in their settings and circumstances, but also in the underwhelming collective responses – money-giving practices aside – that they provoke. Before group belonging is rationalised in its connections to issues deemed of consequence, it is experienced through manipulations of space, material and sound that bring about interpersonal and intergroup co-existence.

While it is understandable that scholars are drawn to exceptional, underground or minority cases, these are not the only musical involvements. Highlighting peak musical happenings may account for the most intensive sense in which experience aggregates through belonging, but in urban situations where music is a largely inescapable backdrop to everyday life, involvements away from these peaks are arguably more prevalent and just as significant. This brings into the foreground the great variety of degrees and qualities with which people engage in the music they encounter in everyday life, with some endorsing and identifying with it and others accepting it passively or even actively disapproving or resisting – that people choose to stop and orientate their bodies along with others in musical aggregations should not be taken for granted and the processes of this differentiation overlooked. Many Passion Square participants may find themselves at these events not because they feel a particular connection to this music above other kinds, but simply because it is what is available in their local area. This study can serve as a reminder, then, that a multiplicity of responses, different degrees of attachment and detachment and a mundane level of personal motivation are also part of musical experiences, just as much as coherent discourses such as those around community tend to promote.

5.4 De-Idealising Community

The notion of community is a driving force in understanding human associations in musical contexts, not to mention in applied ethnomusicology, cultural heritage projects and various other work concerned with making interventions on situations involving people. But it is worth pausing to pay proper scrutiny to how the values that guide scholarship are constructed and harnessed. Being tied so strongly to positive connotations, community is open to the agendas of various kinds of player and this can mean losing sight of the exclusion that is a less intuitively laudable counterpart of belonging. An understanding that takes proper account of the interplay between different modes in real situations can enhance community's meaningfulness as a tool of analysis. Shifting the language of communities to that of community as a quality refocuses on these complexities and dissolves the imperative to see community as a destination (rather than a tool), and a vindication of a certain set of practices or aggregations. Scholarship that de-idealises community reveals what lies behind its rhetoric and it can make the notion meaningful in the contemporary world of everyday musical experiences.

6 List of Songs

The following is a list of all the songs I heard more than once at Passion Square shows in Wuhan in spring and autumn 2014.

Song name	Example recording(s)	
Ai de daijia 爱的代价 The price of love	Zhang Aijia 张艾嘉 1992	Li Zongsheng 李宗盛 2004
Ai de shijie zhi you ni 爱的世界只有你 In the world of love there is only you	Qi Long 祁隆 2013	
Aiqing wanwan sui 爱情万万岁 Long live love	Gao An 高安 2011	
Aiqing zhe bei jiu shei he dou de zui 爱情这杯酒谁喝都得醉 All who drink from the cup of love get intoxicated	Yan Xu 闫旭 2011	
Babai li dongting wo de jia 八百里洞庭我的家 Babai li Dongting, my home	Li Qiong 李琼 1999	
Beijing de jinshan shang 北京的金山上 On Beijing's Jin mountain	Caidan Zhuoma 才旦卓玛 1972	Han Hong 韩红 1998
Boli xin 玻璃心 Heart of glass	Qi Qin 齐秦 1991	
Chuanqi 传奇 Legend	Wang Fei 王菲 2003	
Deng ni dengle name jiu 等你等了那么久 Waited so long for you	Qi Long 祁隆 2012	
Er xing qianli 儿行千里 A son who travels a thousand miles	Li Qiong 李琼 1999	
Fanshen nongnu ba ge chang 翻身农奴把歌唱 The emancipated serf sings	Caidan Zhuoma 才旦卓玛 1954	
Gandong tian gandong di 感动天感动地 Moving heaven, moving the earth	Yu Tongfei 宇桐非 2007	

Song name	Example recording(s)
Ganen de xin 感恩的心 Grateful heart	Ouyang Feifei 欧阳菲菲 1994
Hetang yuese 荷塘月色 Moonlight on the lotus pond	Fenghuang Chuanqi 凤凰传奇 2010
Hongchen qingge 红尘情歌 The ballad of the red dust	Gao An & Hei Yazi 高安 & 黑鸭子 2011
Hongyan 鸿雁 Swan goose	Husileng 呼斯楞 2010
Lao difang de yu 老地方的雨 Rain in the old place	Chen Rui 陈瑞 2014
Lei man tian 泪满天 Tear-filled sky	Long Meizi 龙梅子 2003
Li bu kai ni 离不开你 Can't leave you	Liu Huan 刘欢 1987
Lüdao xiaoyequ 绿岛小夜曲 Green island serenade	Deng Lijun 邓丽君 1976
Meilan meilan wo ai ni 梅兰梅兰我爱你 Merlin, Merlin, I love you	Liu Wenzheng 刘文正 1978
Ni dui wo tai zhongyao 你对我太重要 You are so important to me	T.R.Y. 2006
Qian nian deng yi hui 千年等一回 Waiting a thousand years	Gao Shengmei 高胜美 1992
Qingren 情人 Lover	Huang Pinyuan 黄品源 2004

Song name	Example recording(s)
Qingzang Gaoyuan 青藏高原 The Qinghai-Tibetan Plateau	Han Hong 韩红 2001
Ri bu luo 日不落 The sun doesn't set	Cai Yilin 蔡依林 2007
Ruguo ni ai wo jiu bie shanghai wo 如果你爱我就别伤害我 If you love me don't hurt me	Liu Jialiang 刘嘉亮 2004
Shang bu qi 伤不起 Can't be hurt	Wang Lin 王麟 2011
Shei shi wo de lang 谁是我的郎 Who will be my man	Yang Zi 杨梓 2013
Shenshen de xihuan ni 深深的喜欢你 Liking you deeply	Qiu Niao 囚鸟 2009
Tian lu 天路 Heavenly road	Gong Yue 龚玥 2007
Tian mimi 甜蜜蜜 Sweetheart	Deng Lijun 邓丽君 1979
Wang ning mei 枉凝眉 Love in vain	Chen Li 陈力 1987
Weile shei 为了谁 For whom?	Zu Hai 祖海 1998
Wo ceng yongxin aizhe ni 我曾用心爱着你 I once sincerely loved you	Pan Meichen 潘美辰 1988
Wo shifou ye zai ni xinzhong 我是否也在你心中 Am I in your heart?	Gao An & Qiu Niao 高安 & 囚鸟 2008

Song name	Example recording(s)
Wo yao baozhe ni 我要抱着你 I want to hold you	Pang Long 庞龙 2005
Wo yong ziji de fangshi ai ni 我用自己的方式爱你 I love you in my own way	Chen Mingzhen 陈明真 1991
Wo zhi zaihu ni 我只在乎你 I only care for you	Deng Lijun 邓丽君 1987
Wunai de sixu 无奈的思绪 Helpless mood	Han Baoyi 韩宝仪 1987
Xia yi beizi bu zuo nüren 下一辈子不做女人 Not to be a woman in the next life	Chen Rui 陈瑞 2005
Xiao cheng gushi 小城故事 Small town story	Deng Lijun 邓丽君 1978
Xiao pingguo 小苹果 Little apple	Kuaizi Xiongdi 筷子兄弟 2014
Xiaoxiao de xinniang hua 小小的新娘花 Little bridal flowers	Yun Feifei 云菲菲 2007
Xiangjian wu jishi 相见无几时 Together a short while	Liu Ziling 刘紫玲 2007
Xin zai tiao qing zai shao 心在跳情在烧 Palpitating heart, burning passion	Xie Jun 谢军 2007
Xueshan Ajia 雪山阿佳 A-jia of the snowy mountains	Baima Duoji 白玛多吉 2012
Yi qu xiang song 一曲相送 A song to see you off	Tu Yage 图桠格 2011

Song name	Example recording(s)
Yi sheng wu hui 一生无悔 A lifetime without regret	Gao An & Hang Jiao 高安 & 杭娇 2012
Yuanfen redehuo 缘份惹得祸 Destiny stirring up trouble	An Dongyang 安东阳 2011
Yuelaiyue hao 越来越好 Better and better	Song Zuying 宋祖英 2000
Zai du chong xiangfeng 再度重相逢 Meeting once more	Wu Bai 伍佰 2003
Zhishao hai you ni 至少还有你 At least I still have you	Lin Yilian 林忆莲 2000
Zhizhuo 执着 Persevering	Tian Zhen 田震 1996
Zhu ni ping'an 祝你平安 Wishing you well	Sun Yue 孙悦 1994
Ziyou feixiang 自由飞翔 Flying free	Fenghuang Chuanqi 凤凰传奇 2006
Zou jin xin shidai 走进新时代 Entering a new era	Zhang Ye 张也 1997
Zui xuan minzu feng 最炫民族风 The most dazzling ethnic style	Fenghuang Chuanqi 凤凰传奇 2009
Zuo ni de ai ren 做你的爱人 To be your lover	Rao Tianliang 饶天亮 2006

7 References

Anderson, Benedict (1991). *Imagined Communities: Reflections on the Origin and Spread of Nationalism*, 2nd ed. London: Verso.

Baker, Geoff (2011). 'Cuba Rebelión: Underground Music in Havana', *Latin American Music Review* 32(1): 1–38.

   (2012). 'Mala Bizta Sochal Klu: Underground, Alternative and Commercial in Havana Hip Hop', *Popular Music* 31(1): 1–24.

Baranovitch, Nimrod (2003). *China's New Voices: Popular Music, Ethnicity, Gender and Politics 1978–1997*. Berkeley: University of California Press.

Barber, Karin (1997). 'Preliminary Notes on Audiences in Africa', *Africa* 67(3): 347–62.

Bates, Eliot (2012). 'The Social Life of Musical Instruments', *Ethnomusicology* 56(3): 363–95.

Booth, Gregory and Terry Lee Kuhn (1990). 'Economic and Transmission Factors as Essential Elements in the Definition of Folk, Art, and Pop Music', *Musical Quarterly* 74(3): 411–38.

Boretz, Avron (2004). 'Carousing and Masculinity: The Cultural Production of Gender in Taiwan'. In *Women in the New Taiwan: Gender Roles and Gender Consciousness in a Changing Society*, edited by Catherine Farris, Anru Lee and Murray Rubinstein, pp. 171–98. London: M.E. Sharpe.

Born, Georgina (2013). 'Introduction'. In *Music, Sound and Space: Transformations of Public and Private Experience*, edited by Georgina Born, pp. 1–16. Cambridge: Cambridge University Press.

Chau, Adam Yuet (2008). 'The Sensorial Production of the Social', *Ethnos* 73(4): 485–504.

Chernoff, John (1979). *African Rhythms and African Sensibility: Aesthetics and Social Action in African Musical Idioms*. Chicago: University of Chicago Press.

China News Service (2014). '*Wuhan gongyuan li de "caogen wutai"*' [A Wuhan Park's 'Grassroots Stage']. *Zhongguo xinwen wang*, 3 May 2014, www .chinanews.com/tp/2014/05-03/6126786.shtml (accessed 12 April 2020).

Clayton, Martin (2013). 'Entrainment, Ethnography and Musical Interaction'. In *Experience and Meaning in Music Performance*, edited by Martin Clayton, Byron Dueck and Laura Leante, pp. 17–39. Oxford: Oxford University Press.

   (2017). 'The Ethnography of Embodied Music Interaction'. In *The Routledge Companion to Embodied Music Interaction*, edited by Micheline Lesaffre,

Pieter-Jan Maes and Marc Leman, pp. 215–22. New York and London: Routledge.

Clayton, Martin, Byron Dueck and Laura Leante (2013). 'Introduction: Experience and Meaning in Music Performance'. In *Experience and Meaning in Music Performance*, edited by Martin Clayton, Byron Dueck and Laura Leante, pp. 1–16. Oxford: Oxford University Press.

Cole, Ross (2019). 'On the Politics of Folk Song Theory in Edwardian England', *Ethnomusicology* 63(1): 19–42.

Day, Graham (2006). *Community and Everyday Life*. London: Routledge.

Dueck, Byron (2007). 'Public and Intimate Sociability in First Nations and Métis Fiddling', *Ethnomusicology* 51(1): 30–63.

(2013). *Musical Intimacies and Indigenous Imaginaries: Aboriginal Music and Dance in Public Performance*. New York: Oxford University Press.

Durkheim, Émile ([1893] 1960). *The Division of Labor in Society*. Glencoe: Free Press.

Eisenberg, Andrew (2013). 'Islam, Sound and Space: Acoustemology and Muslim Citizenship on the Kenyan Coast'. In *Music, Sound and Space: Transformations of Public and Private Experience*, edited by Georgina Born, pp. 186–202. Cambridge: Cambridge University Press.

Fairfield, Benjamin (2019). 'Social Synchrony and Tuning Out: Karen Participation in Music, Tradition, and Ethnicity in Northern Thailand', *Ethnomusicology* 63(3): 470–98.

Finnegan, Ruth (1989). *The Hidden Musicians: Music-Making in an English Town*. Cambridge: Cambridge University Press.

Freie, John (1998). *Counterfeit Community: The Exploitation of our Longings for Connectedness*. Lanham: Rowman & Littlefield.

García Quiñones, Marta, Anahid Kassabian and Elena Boschi, eds. (2016). *Ubiquitous Musics: The Everyday Sounds that We Don't Always Notice*. London: Routledge.

Graezer, Florence (2004). 'Breathing New Life into Beijing Culture: New "Traditional" Public Spaces and the Chaoyang Neighbourhood Yangge Associations'. In *Making Place: State Projects, Globalisation and Local Responses in China*, edited by Stephan Feuchtwang, pp. 61–78. London: UCL.

Gusfield, Joseph (1975). *Community: A Critical Response*. Oxford: Blackwell.

Habermas, Jürgen (1989). *The Structural Transformation of the Public Sphere: An Inquiry into a Category of Bourgeois Society*. Oxford: Polity.

Hao Xiaoyan, Wang Xiaowu and Yin Huazhang (2005). '*Jiangbian youyuan qidai zhengzhi "zangluancha"*' [Riverside Park Awaiting Restoration of Messy

Environment]. *Chujing wang Chutian dushi bao*, 3 January 2005, http://news .sina.com.cn/s/2005-01-03/07134700623s.shtml (accessed 29 October 2020).

Harris, Rachel (2020). '"A Weekly Mäshräp to Tackle Extremism": Music-Making in Uyghur Communities and Intangible Cultural Heritage in China', *Ethnomusicology* 64(1): 23–55.

Harrison-Pepper, Sally ([1990] 2010). *Drawing a Circle in the Square: Street Performing in New York's Washington Square Park*. London: University Press of Mississippi.

Herrera, Eduardo (2018). 'Masculinity, Violence, and Deindividuation in Argentine Soccer Chants: The Sonic Potentials of Participatory Sounding-in-Synchrony', *Ethnomusicology* 62(3): 470–99.

Hirschkind, Charles (2006). *The Ethical Soundscape: Cassette Sermons and Islamic Counterpublics*. New York: University of Columbia Press.

Horlor, Samuel (2019a). 'Neutralizing Temporary Inequities in Moral Status: Chinese Street Singers and the Gift Economy', *Asian Music* 50 (2): 3–32.

(2019b). 'Permeable Frames: Intersections of the Performance, the Everyday, and the Ethical in Chinese Street Singing', *Ethnomusicology Forum* 28(1): 3–25.

(2019c). 'Chinese Street Pop and Performing with the Urban Environment', *Sound Ethnographies* 2(1): 39–68.

Impey, Angela (2002). 'Culture, Conservation and Community Reconstruction: Explorations in Advocacy Ethnomusicology and Participatory Action Research in Northern Kwazulu Natal', *Yearbook for Traditional Music* 34: 9–24.

Jankowiak, William (1993). *Sex, Death, and Hierarchy in a Chinese City: An Anthropological Account*. New York: Columbia University Press.

Jones, Stephen (2013). 'Gender and Music in Local Communities'. In *Gender in Chinese Music*, edited by Rachel Harris, Rowan Pease and Shzr Ee Tan, pp. 26–40. Rochester: University of Rochester Press.

Ju Di (2014). '*Fuqi jianghan lu maichang jiu zi chengguan youqing zhifa zhu qi zhuanchang jiangtan*' [Couple Sell their Song at Jianghan Lu, City Management Enforce Law with Compassion, Assist with Move to River Beach]. *Changjiang wang*, 16 May 2014, http://news.cjn.cn/sywh/201405/ t2473134.htm (accessed 12 April 2020).

Kendall, Paul (2019). *The Sounds of Social Space: Branding, Built Environment, and Leisure in Urban China*. Honolulu: University of Hawai'i Press.

Kendon, Adam (1990). *Conducting Interaction: Patterns of Behavior in Focused Encounters*. Cambridge: Cambridge University Press.

Kenny, Ailbhe (2016). *Communities of Musical Practice*. Abingdon: Routledge.

King, Ambrose Y.C. (1985). 'The Individual and Group in Confucianism: A Relational Perspective'. In *Individualism and Holism: Studies in Confucian and Taoist Values*, edited by Donald Munro, pp. 57–70. Ann Arbor: University of Michigan.

Komlosy, Anouska (2008). 'Yunnanese Sounds: Creativity and Alterity in the Dance and Music Scenes of Urban Yunnan', *China: An International Journal* 6(1): 44–68.

Kreutzfeld, Jacob (2010). 'Acoustic Territoriality and the Politics of Urban Noise', *Soundscape* 10(1): 14–17.

Krims, Adam (2007). *Music and Urban Geography*. New York: Routledge.

LaBelle, Brandon (2010). *Acoustic Territories: Sound Culture and Everyday Life*. New York and London: Continuum.

Landau, Carolyn (2012). 'Disseminating Music amongst Moroccans in Britain: Exploring the Value of Archival Sound Recordings for a Cultural Heritage Community in the Diaspora', *Ethnomusicology Forum* 21(2): 259–77.

Latour, Bruno (1996). 'On Actor-Network Theory: A Few Clarifications', *Soziale Welt* 47(4): 369–81.

Lau, Frederick (1991). *Music and Musicians of the Traditional Chinese 'Dizi' in the People's Republic of China*. Ann Arbor: University Microfilms International.

Lee, Tong Soon (1999). 'Technology and the Production of Islamic Public Space: The Call to Prayer in Singapore', *Ethnomusicology* 43(1): 86–100.

Lena, Jennifer C. (2012). *Banding Together: How Communities Create Genres in Popular Music*. Princeton: Princeton University Press.

Lucas, Glaura, Martin Clayton and Laura Leante (2011). 'Inter-Group Entrainment in Afro-Brazilian Congado Ritual', *Empirical Musicology Review* 6(2): 75–102.

Lum, Casey Man Kong (1996). *In Search of a Voice: Karaoke and the Construction of Identity in Chinese America*. Mahwah: Lawrence Erlbaum Associates.

McGuire, Colin P. (2018). 'Unisonance in Kung Fu Film Music, or the Wong Fei-hung Theme Song as a Cantonese Transnational Anthem', *Ethnomusicology Forum* 27(1): 48–67.

Mitsui, Tōru and Shūhei Hosokawa (1998). 'Introduction'. In *Karaoke around the World: Global Technology, Local Singing*, edited by Tōru Mitsui and Shūhei Hosokawa, pp. 1–26. London: Routledge.

Moskowitz, Marc (2010). *Cries of Joy, Songs of Sorrow: Chinese Pop Music and its Cultural Connotations*. Honolulu: University of Hawai'i Press.

O'Grady, Lucy and Katrina McFerran (2007). 'Community Music Therapy and Its Relationship to Community Music: Where Does It End?', *Nordic Journal of Music Therapy* 16(1): 14–26.

O'Shea, Helen (2007). 'Getting to the Heart of the Music: Idealizing Musical Community and Irish Traditional Music Sessions', *Journal of the Society for Musicology in Ireland* 2: 1–18.

Parmar, Robin (2019). 'Sounding the Anthropocene: Rethinking Soundscapes and Nature', online research paper, http://robinparmar.com/paper-sound ing-the-anthropocene.html (accessed 20 April 2020).

Pelczynski, Zbigniew (1984). 'Introduction: The Significance of Hegel's Separation of the State and Civil Society'. In *The State and Civil Society: Studies in Hegel's Political Philosophy*, edited by Zbigniew Pelczynski, pp. 1–13. Cambridge: Cambridge University Press.

Post, Jennifer C. (2007). '"I Take My Dombra and Sing to Remember my Homeland": Identity, Landscape and Music in Kazakh Communities of Western Mongolia', *Ethnomusicology Forum* 16(1): 45–69.

Ramnarine, Tina K. (2011). 'The Orchestration of Civil Society: Community and Conscience in Symphony Orchestras', *Ethnomusicology Forum* 20(3): 327–51.

Rees, Helen (2016). 'Environmental Crisis, Culture Loss, and a New Musical Aesthetic: China's "Original Ecology Folksongs" In Theory and Practice', *Ethnomusicology* 60(1): 53–88.

Revill, George (2005). 'Vernacular Culture and the Place of Folk Music', *Social & Cultural Geography* 6(5): 693–706.

Rowe, William (1984). *Hankow: Commerce and Society in a Chinese City, 1796–1889*. Stanford: Stanford University Press.

(1989). *Hankow: Conflict and Community in a Chinese City, 1796–1895*. Stanford: Stanford University Press.

(1990). 'The Public Sphere in Modern China', *Modern China* 16(3): 309–29.

Schafer, R. Murray (1977). *The Tuning of the World*. New York: Alfred A. Knopf.

Schechner, Richard (1988). *Performance Theory*, rev. and expanded ed. Routledge: New York and London.

Seetoo, Chiayi and Haoping Zou (2016). 'China's Guangchang Wu: The Emergence, Choreography, and Management of Dancing in Public Squares', *TDR/The Drama Review* 60(4): 22–49.

Shelemay, Kay Kaufman (2011). 'Musical Communities: Rethinking the Collective in Music', *Journal of the American Musicological Society* 64 (2): 349–90.

Shue, Vivienne (1995). 'State Sprawl: The Regulatory State and Social Life in a Small Chinese City'. In *Urban Spaces in Contemporary China: The Potential for Autonomy and Community in Post-Mao China*, edited by Deborah Davis, Richard Kraus, Barry Naughton and Elizabeth Perry, pp. 90–112. Cambridge: Cambridge University Press.

Stock, Jonathan (2002). *Huju: Traditional Opera in Modern Shanghai*. Oxford: Oxford University Press.

Stockman, Norman (2000). *Understanding Chinese Society*. Cambridge: Polity.

Stokes, Martin (1994). 'Introduction: Ethnicity, Identity and Music'. In *Ethnicity, Identity and Music: The Musical Construction of Place*, edited by Martin Stokes, pp. 1–27. Oxford: Berg.

Taylor, Timothy (2007). 'The Commodification of Music at the Dawn of the Era of "Mechanical Music"', *Ethnomusicology* 51(2): 281–305.

Titon, Jeff Todd (2015). 'Exhibiting Music in a Sound Community', *Ethnologies* 37(1): 23–41.

Titon, Jeff Todd and Svanibor Pettan (2015). 'An Introduction to Applied Ethnomusicology'. In *The Oxford Handbook of Applied Ethnomusicology*, edited by Svanibor Pettan and Jeff Todd Titon, pp. 3–68. Oxford: Oxford University Press.

Tönnies, Ferdinand ([1887] 2001). *Community and Civil Society*, edited by Jose Harris, translated by Jose Harris and Margaret Hollis. Cambridge: Cambridge University Press.

Torp, Claudius (2017). 'Missionary Education and Musical Communities in Sub-Saharan Colonial Africa', *Itinerario* 41(2): 235–51.

Truax, Barry ([1984] 2001). *Acoustic Communication*. Westport: Ablex.

Tuan, Yi-fu (1982). *Segmented Worlds and Self: Group Life and Individual Consciousness*. Minneapolis: University of Minnesota Press.

Turino, Thomas (2008). *Music as Social Life: The Politics of Participation*. Chicago: University of Chicago Press.

Turner, Victor (1969). *The Ritual Process: Structure and Anti-Structure*. London: Routledge & Kegan Paul.

UNESCO (2018). *Basic Texts of the 2003 Convention for the Safeguarding of the Intangible Cultural Heritage*. Paris: UNESCO, https://ich.unesco.org/doc/src/2003_Convention_Basic_Texts-_2018_version-EN.pdf (accessed 26 October 2020).

Wakeman, Frederic (1993). 'The Civil Society and Public Sphere Debate: Western Reflections on Chinese Political Culture', *Modern China* 19(2): 108–38.

Wang Ying-Fen (2003). 'Amateur Music Clubs and State Intervention: The Case of *Nanguan* Music in Postwar Taiwan', *Journal of Chinese Ritual, Theatre and Folklore* 141: 95–167.

Warner, Michael (2002). 'Publics and Counterpublics', *Public Culture* 14(1): 49–90.

Wenger, Etienne (1998). *Communities of Practice: Learning, Meaning and Identity*. Cambridge: Cambridge University Press.

Wu Cuncun (2004). *Homoerotic Sensibilities in Late Imperial China*. Abingdon: RoutledgeCurzon.

Xu Feng (2008). 'New Modes of Urban Governance: Building Community/ *Shequ* in Post-*Danwei* China'. In *The Chinese Party-State in the 21st Century: Adaptation and the Reinvention of Legitimacy*, edited by André Laliberté, and Marc Lanteigne, pp. 22–38. London and New York: Routledge.

Yang, Mayfair Mei-hui (1994). *Gifts, Favors, and Banquets: The Art of Social Relationships in China*. Ithaca: Cornell University Press.

Yuan Chunlin (2014). '*Huajia fuqi wanju juankuan jietou maichang jiu zi*' [Retired Couple Gracefully Declines Donations, Performs on Street to Save Son]. *Daqing wang*, 6 May 2014, www.dqdaily.com/shishi/2014-05/16/content_2042911.htm (accessed 24 February 2016).

Zhang, Wenzhao (2020). 'Tonight, We Are All Wuhan-ers: Reimagining Urban Subjectivities, Space, and Music Healing', *Association for Chinese Music Research Newsletter* 25(1): 13–16, https://evols.library.manoa.hawaii.edu/handle/10524/63250 (accessed 27 October 2020).

Zhou Xun and Francesca Tarocco (2007). *Karaoke: The Global Phenomenon*. London: Reaktion.

Elements in Twenty-First Century Music Practice

Simon Zagorski-Thomas
London College of Music, University of West London

Simon Zagorski-Thomas is a Professor at the London College of Music (University of West London, UK) and founded and runs the 21st Century Music Practice Research Network. He is series editor for the Cambridge Elements series and Bloomsbury book series on 21st Century Music Practice. He is ex-chairman and co-founder of the Association for the Study of the Art of Record Production. He is a composer, sound engineer and producer and is, currently, writing a monograph on practical musicology. His books include *Musicology of Record Production* (2014; winner of the 2015 IASPM Book Prize), *The Art of Record Production: an Introductory Reader for a New Academic Field* co-edited with Simon Frith (2012), the *Bloomsbury Handbook of Music Production* co-edited with Andrew Bourbon (2020) and the *Art of Record Production: Creative Practice in the Studio* co-edited with Katia Isakoff, Serge Lacasse and Sophie Stévance (2020).

About the Series

Elements in Twenty-First Century Music Practice has developed out of the 21st Century Music Practice Research Network, which currently has around 250 members in 30 countries and is dedicated to the study of what Christopher Small termed musicking – the process of making and sharing music rather than the output itself. Obviously this exists at the intersection of ethnomusicology, performance studies, and practice pedagogy / practice-led-research in composition, performance, recording, production, musical theatre, music for screen and other forms of multi-media musicking. The generic nature of the term '21st Century Music Practice' reflects the aim of the series to bring together all forms of music into a larger discussion of current practice and to provide a platform for research about any musical tradition or style. It embraces everything from hip-hop to historically informed performance and K-pop to Inuk throat singing.

Cambridge Elements ≡

Elements in Twenty-First Century Music Practice

Elements in the Series

The Marks of a Maestro: Annotating Mozart's 'Jupiter' Symphony
Raymond Holden and Stephen Mould

Chinese Street Music: Complicating Musical Community
Samuel Horlor

A full series listing is available at: www.cambridge.org/emup

Printed in the United States
by Baker & Taylor Publisher Services